Restore Unity, Recover Identity, Refine Orthopraxy

Restore Unity, Recover Identity, Refine Orthopraxy

The Believers' Priesthood in the Ecclesiology of James Leo Garrett Jr.

Peter L. Tie

WIPF & STOCK · Eugene, Oregon

RESTORE UNITY, RECOVER IDENTITY, REFINE ORTHOPRAXY
The Believers' Priesthood in the Ecclesiology of James Leo Garrett Jr.

Copyright © 2012 Peter Tie. All rights reserved. Except for brief quotations in critical publications or reviews, no part of this book may be reproduced in any manner without prior written permission from the publisher. Write: Permissions, Wipf and Stock Publishers, 199 W. 8th Ave., Suite 3, Eugene, OR 97401.

Wipf & Stock
An imprint of Wipf and Stock Publishers
199 W. 8th Ave., Suite 3
Eugene, OR 97401

www.wipfandstock.com

ISBN 13: 978-1-61097-789-0

Manufactured in the U.S.A.

To
My lovely wife, Ruth,
and
Our three beautiful children,
Anastasia, Timothy, Annabelle

Contents

Foreword by David S. Dockery / ix

Preface / xiii

chapter 1
Introduction to Garrett's Ecclesiology / 1

chapter 2
The Mission of the Church / 21

chapter 3
The Membership of the Church / 42

chapter 4
The Ministry of the Church / 65

chapter 5
The Management of the Church / 90

chapter 6
Garrett's Important Motifs in Perspective / 114

Bibliography / 123

Foreword

THE WELL-RESEARCHED VOLUME BY Peter Tie, which you hold in your hands, is a much-welcomed contribution to the study of Baptist theology in general and to the field of ecclesiology in particular. Moreover, *Restore Unity, Recover Identity, Refine Orthopraxy* provides us with a masterful understanding of the key elements in the theological proposals offered by the most knowledgeable historical theologian in Baptist life over the past sixty years, James Leo Garrett Jr. A little more than thirty years ago I walked into a theology class as a young seminary student at Southwestern Baptist Theological Seminary. This class, taught by Professor Garrett, changed the way that I thought about theology and theological method, and has greatly shaped the way I have approached the study of the history of biblical interpretation, the development of Christian doctrine, and the entire Christian intellectual tradition. My story can be amplified by dozens and dozens of others.

The tributes to Garrett's influential work have been many throughout his long teaching career, which has stretched over a half-century at Southwestern Baptist Theological Seminary, Southern Baptist Theological Seminary, and Baylor University, in addition to numerous special lectureships and visiting professorships at a variety of campuses in the United States and around the globe. Through his rigorous classes and seminars, as well as his thorough, prolific, and influential writings, Garrett's endeavors have introduced several student generations to the historical depth and breadth of the Christian faith. As important as Garrett's work has been in the area of historical theology, his theological contributions to Baptist life and thought have been equally significant, if not even more so. In 1991, several of Garrett's friends, colleagues, and former students attempted to acknowledge Garrett's vast contribution to Baptist thought and Christian ecclesiology with a volume of essays published in his honor on his sixty-fifth birthday. This volume, *People of God: Essays on the Believers' Church*, explored the themes and expanded the proposals so prominent in Garrett's work. Picking up on those themes, Peter Tie has examined carefully the marvelous insights regarding the believers' priesthood in Garrett's theological contributions, particularly found in his ecclesiological articulations.

I am enthusiastic about this new volume by Peter Tie. I believe that he has captured well the essence and distinctive contributions advanced in the writings of Professor Garrett. In many ways the study of the church, which is the central theme in Tie's volume, has been the most neglected area of theological study. It has certainly been the area in which the most diverse theological viewpoints have been found, hence the multitude of Christian denominations and denominational distinctions. While there is vast agreement that the church is the community of men and women who have received God's gift of salvation, both widely-known and less-pronounced differences remain regarding the order, organization, and missional directives for the people of God, not to mention matters related to worship, ministry, discipline, the ordinances or sacraments, fellowship, outreach, service, and mission.

While agreement exists that the church is God's church in both origin and end, the multisided images and multiple models of the church found in the New Testament reflect much variety in the understanding of the life and work of the church. Some of these images include the church as the fellowship of the Holy Spirit (Phil 2:2), the new creation (Eph 2:15), the household of God (Gal 6:10), the pillar of truth (1 Tim 3:15), the body of Christ (Eph 1:22), and the bride of Christ (Rev 19:17). The idea of the church as the people of God pictures its universality, crossing all segments of society (Gal 3:28). The image of the new creation portrays Christ's victory over evil as a new humanity in the midst of the fallen world. The household of God points to the visible form of God's people who relate to one another in community and constitute the new creation. The body of Christ shows the presence of Christ in the world. Focusing only on one of these pictures or models, Christians through the centuries have presented various trajectories of what the church should be and do, differing over the mission, membership, ministry, and management of the church.

Peter Tie, beautifully reflecting both the spirit and insights of James Leo Garrett Jr., has reminded us that the church is more than a human organization. The church of the Lord Jesus Christ is a visible and tangible expression of the people who are in Christ and who are related to one another in Christ. With a focus on the concept of the priesthood of believers, Tie invites Christ-followers to reconsider the primacy of the church, to refine its orthopraxy, to recover its identity, and to restore its unity. Tie clearly recognizes that the church has a dual purpose in the world: it is to be a holy priesthood (1 Pet 2:5), while also declaring the wonderful deeds of God, who called the believing community out of darkness into the marvelous light made known in the gospel message (1 Pet 2:9).

The value of Peter Tie's work is also twofold. First, it introduces readers to the vast writings of James Leo Garrett Jr. Perhaps more importantly, it provides readers with a fresh perspective regarding the important field of ecclesiology. With insightful engagement of both biblical and historical material, Tie points readers toward a balanced, biblical, and Baptist understanding of theology and the church. I trust that many readers will be blessed and encouraged, even as I have been, by the proposal and analytical thought offered in this volume through the pen of Peter Tie.

Soli Deo Gloria.

David S. Dockery
President, Union University

Preface

Teaching Christian doctrines has been my calling and passion but not without challenges. I remember distinctly when I first started preparing for the lectures on systematic theology to a group of graduate students in a Malaysian seminary. The preparation seemed to go rather smoothly until I reached the doctrine of the church. I was at a loss because many theological textbooks that I consulted were filled with various theories and a multitude of controversies, leaving me with a sense of helplessness, as if I were drowned in a pool of uncertainty, disunity, and impracticality. From there began my journey to search for an adequate ecclesiology.

Through the doctoral seminar on "Baptist Theologians" taught by Dr. Malcolm Yarnell, I was introduced to the ecclesiological writings of Dr. James Leo Garrett Jr., a well-respected Southern Baptist theologian and distinguished professor of Southwestern Baptist Theological Seminary. At the time, two distinctive features of Garrett's ecclesiology grasped my attention: first, his continuous efforts to promote Christian unity while at the same time rediscovering Baptist identity and distinctives; second, his intentional gesture of placing the chapter on the church's mission almost at the forefront of the ecclesiology in his *Systematic Theology*. These features prompted me to dig deeper and look further with the hope of ascertaining a biblically balanced ecclesiology. My research yields this present monograph.

The completion of this book is only possible through the time well spent in conversations and discussions with Dr. Garrett. He earned my utmost respect for his profound knowledge and humble heart. Dr. Yarnell, my PhD advisor, supervisor, and role model, who always keeps his theological erudition and spiritual maturity in balance, is the major reason for the completion of this monograph. I extend my sincere gratitude to Dr.

Yarnell for teaching me how to think theologically and write effectively. I am also truly appreciative of Dr. Dongsun Cho for his timely advice, scholarly comments, and constant support. Dr. David S. Dockery, who took time from his busy schedule as the president of the Union University to read through this monograph and to write its foreword, is such an inspiration and encouragement. Thank you from the bottom of my heart.

Special thanks to my proofreaders, Tamra Hernandez, Helen Dent, Peter Ho, Suresh Vythylingam, and Joseph Wright, who made this book presentable and readable. My heartfelt thanks to each one of them! God alone has seen my family's love, patience, and sacrifices during my entire writing process. May the gracious God reward them manifoldly for their persistent prayers and partnership. This book is dedicated to my family.

Last but not least, I am truly grateful to Wipf & Stock for publishing my PhD dissertation. May the Holy Spirit use this monograph to enlighten, edify, and empower the people of God, i.e., the royal priesthood.

chapter 1

Introduction to Garrett's Ecclesiology

INTRODUCTION TO THE ISSUE

ECCLESIOLOGY IS ALLEGEDLY ONE of the theological foci that brings much confusion, conflict, or controversy within the church. Ironically, James Leo Garrett, Distinguished Professor of Theology Emeritus of Southwestern Baptist Theological Seminary, perceives that the much neglected and avoided doctrine of the church is the place where the churches may restore unity, recover identity, and refine orthopraxy.

Garrett is known by his fellow theologians as the "most knowledgeable Baptist theologian living today,"[1] or simply, among his students, as the "walking theological encyclopedia." He is first and foremost a Baptist historical theologian seeking to discover or recover the Baptist identity vis-à-vis other Christian groups. His strength lies primarily in historical theology and secondarily in systematic theology and biblical exegesis. Although many of his works are historical in nature, his learned contributions cannot be ignored. He may not be considered as one of the most creative or innovative theologians, but his constant writing on ecclesiological themes, in particular, has been a significant and steady influence in the Baptist world.

Garrett has always been interested in various ecclesiological topics, initially due to his historical contexts and later due to his theological convictions. Prompted by the ecumenical movement, Garrett deems

---

1. Basden, "James Leo Garrett Jr.," 298.

ecclesiology as the most crucial issue not just for theological scholarship but also for ecclesial praxis.[2] Throughout nearly sixty years of teaching, Garrett explored and explicated at one time or another some much neglected as well as controversial aspects of the church, such as: the nature of the church; the unity of the Christian churches (i.e., Christian ecumenism); the concept of the believers' church; believer's baptism by immersion; regenerate church membership; church discipline; the church-state relations; Christian mission; and the doctrine of the priesthood of all believers.

In 1991, a festschrift in honor of Garrett rightly perceived that the doctrine of the church is the primary focus of Garrett, who has led many Baptists back to this ecclesiological center. The festschrift appeared before the second volume of Garrett's *Systematic Theology* (1995), and so his ecclesiology therein. It is, therefore, to their credit that the contributors of the festschrift identified correctly that ecclesiology is Garrett's central interest. More than twenty-five prominent biblical, theological, and historical scholars contributed twenty-five chapters on a variety of topics pertaining to the church, but none seems to address why Garrett has been so concerned with ecclesiology, or even more importantly, what actually drives Garrett's ecclesiology; namely, what is the unifying theme of Garrett's diverse issues of the church?[3]

Garrett's dealings with various ecclesiological topics at first glance appear to be indiscriminate in contents and indecisive in conclusions, but they, under a careful scrutiny, consistently revolve around a crucial theological principle. This book, therefore, attempts to demonstrate that the doctrine of the priesthood of all believers is a unifying motif in Garrett's ecclesiology, as will be seen in the major aspects of his ecclesiology. To identify his central theological motif is to integrate Garrett's ecclesiology as expressed in his multifaceted treatments of the church. To discern and determine his unifying theme, on the other hand, may help discover a distinctively Baptist, biblical, and balanced ecclesiology.

2. Garrett, "Ecclesiology: The Crucial Issue," 14 October 1954, 6–7; 21 October 1954, 8.

3. Basden and Dockery, eds., *People of God*, ix. Garrett points out to this writer that William Pitts studied Garrett's writing on Christian unity or ecumenism in detail (part 3, chapter 17). Others, however, did not deal directly with Garrett's writings on church discipline, priesthood of all believers, or believers' baptism, to mention a few, the topics that he had written substantially or treated significantly even before the publication of his *Systematic Theology* (Vol. 2, 1995).

THESIS STATED AND EXPLAINED

This monograph will argue that the priesthood of all believers is a unifying motif that embodies Garrett's ecclesiological themes as well as establishes his overall ecclesiology. The influence of Garrett's doctrine of the Christian priesthood upon his general ecclesiology is palpably perceived in his writings on the mission, membership, ministry, and management of the church.

Retrospectively, the doctrine of the church was initially the place where Martin Luther, Ulrich Zwingli, and John Calvin were divided, specifically, over the nature of the Lord's Supper or the Eucharist. All of them agreed on the fact that Christ instituted the Lord's Supper for the church or Christians and all are to observe the event, but the Reformers parted on its meaning or nature and, subsequently, its pastoral implications.[4] It was the earliest indication that, first, the disunity of the church begins within the doctrine of the church; and that, second, the tension between doctrine and practice becomes a crucial and perennial issue in ecclesiology.[5] For Garrett, however, ecclesiology is the realm where Christian churches are supposed to restore unity, as well as where faith and life are to unite, a place where orthodoxy and orthopraxy become possible and real.[6]

The sixteenth-century Reformers were known more for the discovery of the biblical doctrine of justification by faith, but less for the recovery of the biblical teaching of the priesthood of Christians. In fact, the two doctrines are foundational to all Christians and churches. Justification by

---

4. Luther, *Martin Luther's Basic Theological Writings*, 277–80. The Marburg Colloquy (1529) was an attempt for a Protestant cooperation at the time. Luther and Zwingli agreed on the first fourteen articles of faith written mainly by Luther, but disagreed on the fifteenth article (on the Lord's Supper), whether the body and blood of Christ in the bread and wine were "bodily" or "symbolic." Calvin, standing between Luther's "bodily" view and Zwingli's "symbolic" view, argued for a "spiritual" view; namely, Christ is present in the Supper by the act of the Holy Spirit, while the resurrected body of Christ remains in heaven. See Calvin, *Institutes*, 359–60, 366–67, 369, 377–78, 389–90, 397–99.

5. The "Lord's Supper" controversy was fundamentally a Christological issue that, nonetheless, had an immediate impact on the unity of the Reformers—Luther, Zwingli, and Calvin. The fact that Garrett approaches the Lord's Supper within the context of church unity suggests that he treats the doctrine primarily from an ecclesiological perspective, without, definitely, discounting the Christological disputes on the Lord's Supper. See Garrett, *Systematic Theology*, 2:659–87. Unless indicated otherwise, this book uses the second edition of Garrett's two-volume *Systematic Theology*.

6. Garrett, *Systematic Theology*, 1:5; 2:659, 685.

faith is the basis of soteriology, whereas the universal priesthood is the foundation of ecclesiology. The former emphasizes the individual life, the latter stresses the corporate life; the former is concerned with the faith in the true gospel, the latter with the common life of true disciples. Timothy George rightly notes that Luther's greatest contribution to the churches was the doctrine of the royal priesthood of all believers, which, unfortunately through subsequent individualistic interpretations, has become a cause of great confusion among Christians.[7] Some take the doctrine to mean the total abolition of church leadership; others the right of private interpretation of Scripture, doctrine, or practice; still others the right of individual voting in church business; and others the privilege of private worship, even the reason or excuse for omitting corporate worship. The doctrine of the royal priesthood has become the catalyst for "subjectivism, eccentricity, anarchy, and chaos."[8] The central element of ecclesiology seems to have become the greatest enemy to the churches.

Garrett is convinced, however, that the biblical understanding and appreciation of the universal priesthood is a potentially powerful means for church renewal, both in doctrine and practice. Throughout this book, one will see that the priesthood of all believers in Garrett's ecclesiology is a theological foundation not only to unify his diverse ecclesiological topics, but also to unite spiritually, rather than institutionally, the worldwide Christian churches, as well as ultimately to bring together the matter of doctrine (believing) and discipleship (living). Stated concisely, Garrett's doctrine of the church rooted in the universal priesthood is to unite and distinguish, rather than to divide and extinguish.

To argue that the priesthood of all believers is a central, guiding, unifying motif of Garrett's ecclesiology does not mean that the priesthood

---

7. George, *Theology of the Reformers*, 95.
8. Eastwood, *Priesthood of All Believers*, 80.

doctrine is his "sole motif"[9] or the "mother principle"[10] in the sense that without it all other ecclesial themes disintegrate, or with it *alone* Garrett develops and interprets other ecclesial aspects. This monograph will primarily argue that the doctrine of the universal priesthood is an essential, foundational, or unifying concept for Garrett's ecclesiology because, as the chapters will show, virtually all of Garrett's ecclesial aspects consistently revolve around or point to the character and function of the Christian priesthood. Moreover, the book will reveal that the "Trinitarian" theme and the "discipleship" motif also play an indispensably supportive role in Garrett's overall ecclesiology.

DELIMITATIONS AND CHALLENGES

The goal of this book is not to survey the historical development of the doctrine of the believers' priesthood, nor to exegete the biblical passages pertaining to such a doctrine, nor to formulate a comprehensive priesthood doctrine for the church of Christ.[11] Rather, while acknowledging that the historical, biblical, systematic, and practical elements of the doctrine will be discussed sporadically throughout the book, this writer primarily intends to demonstrate that Garrett's notion of the priesthood of all believers pervades all of his major ecclesiological themes; promotes Christian unity among the churches while defining Baptist distinctives;

---

9. Norman, "Southern Baptist Identity," 44–45, 57. Norman uses the term "sole" to describe the supremacy and sufficiency of Scripture as the ultimate source for religious authority, belief, and practice. As consistently found in virtually all Baptist writings, Scripture functions as the "core" organizing principle for developing and interpreting other doctrines. Garrett definitely concurs with this "sole" and material principle of the ultimate truthfulness and supreme authority of Scripture. See Garrett, *Systematic Theology*, 1:5–8, 118–20, 183–85. Thus, in this sense, it would be theologically inappropriate to argue that the royal priesthood doctrine is the "sole" principle for the development or interpretation of Garrett's overall ecclesiology.

10. Yarnell, "Changing Baptist Concepts of Royal Priesthood," 245. Yarnell uses the term "mother principle" to describe E. Y. Mullins's notion of "soul competency" as the sole lynchpin of all other theological themes and the governing lens for the interpretation of other doctrines.

11. For recent publications or reprints on the priesthood doctrine from biblical, historical, theological, and/or pastoral perspectives, see Eastwood, *Priesthood of All Believers*; Eastwood, *Royal Priesthood of the Faithful*; Leithart, *Priesthood of the Plebs*; Muthiah, *Priesthood of All Believers*; O'Collins and Jones, *Jesus Our Priests*; Ogden, *Unfinished Business*; Torrance, *Royal Priesthood*; Wengert, *Priesthood, Pastors, Bishops*; Yarnell, "Royal Priesthood in the English Reformation."

and preserves the intimate relation between orthodoxy (correct doctrine) and orthopraxy (correct deed).

The attempt to argue for a unifying motif in Garrett's ecclesiology is not without challenges. Garrett is not always explicit with his theological positions, especially on controversial issues. As noted, he is primarily a historical theologian; therefore, his writings frequently contain expansive treatments of historical figures on various theological subjects. As a careful and thorough historical theologian, he does not leave any stone unturned. He is able to muster "various historical positions on a given theological issue" without necessarily articulating his own positions or proposing specific solutions.[12] Consequently, it is difficult, though not impossible, to discern or determine Garrett's personal views on particular ecclesial issues.

A further problem ensues as Garrett's references to various scriptural texts, historical facts, and theological statements often seem to fall short of in-depth analysis, wholesome interactions, or integrated perspectives, despite the fact that he is indisputably capable of collecting innumerable biblical, historical, and doctrinal materials for a given doctrine. Morrison accuses Garrett of not placing the diverse data into "interactive or interrelated wholes. The many elements tend to sit side by side like lumps and thus often read like lists of statements, beliefs and positions without any clear welding element giving that needed wholeness and directional, interpretive unity."[13] The lack of correlativity may create complexity to the search for a unifying theme in Garrett's ecclesiology. Thus, in view of the challenges posed before this present writer, the research of this monograph mandates painstaking assessment and, particularly, workable methodology.

METHODOLOGY

In order to argue for Garrett's ecclesiology as rooted in the universal priesthood of believers, this writer will begin in the latter half of this first chapter by providing an overall picture of Garrett's rediscovery and redefinition of the common priesthood in relation to his ecclesiology. Only

---

12. Brand, review of *Systematic Theology*, 523–24. Brand assesses: "It is quite clear that he [Garrett] does stand within the evangelical, orthodox Baptist tradition. But he is less concerned to contend for 'answers' than he is to explicate 'options.'"

13. Morrison, "Trinity and Church," 451.

then is one ready to summarize Garrett's numerous themes of the church under distinct categories and chapters based on his writings directly related to ecclesiology: the mission (chapter 2), membership (chapter 3), ministry (chapter 4), and management (chapter 5) of the church.

After exploring each category, critical evaluations will be offered in each chapter in light of the character or function of the priesthood of all believers. In the process of evaluation, this writer attempts to discern and ascertain the major motifs in Garrett's ecclesiology by means of interactions with selected contemporary ecclesiologists from various Christian traditions, especially those whose writings manifest Trinitarian, priesthood, and/or discipleship themes of ecclesiology, namely, Herschel Hobbs, Robert Muthiah, Lesslie Newbigin, Peter Leithart, Miroslav Volf, John Hammett, Hans Küng, Walter Shurden, Stanley Grenz, David Dockery, Malcolm Yarnell, John Yoder, and Avery Dulles, wherever and whenever deemed appropriate. This framework of interactions with other recent ecclesiologists of different Christian traditions—Roman Catholic, Reformed, Baptist, Mennonite, and other Free Church—helps illuminate Garrett's unifying motif behind his various ecclesiological themes. It is preliminarily observed that while the notion of the triune God is an important and implicit motif, Garrett's essential and explicit motif lies in the priesthood of all believers, a doctrinal basis that necessarily implies the motif of discipleship.

OUTLINE

After providing a delineation of Garrett's overall view on the Christian priesthood in chapter 1, chapter 2 explores the theme of the mission of the church by providing a synopsis as well as an analysis of Garrett's major writings on Christian mission to demonstrate that they revolve around the basic concept of the priesthood of all believers. The mission of the church is one of the earliest and major concerns in Garrett's theological vocation. He rightly observes that many Baptist authors of systematic theology usually omitted the crucial subject of Christian world mission.[14] Garrett is one of the first two Baptist theologians to devote a full chapter on church mission in his *Systematic Theology* to show that church evangelization is an essential doctrine and function of the church.[15] Subsequently, he

14. Garrett, "Missions and Baptist Systematic Theologies," 67.
15. The other is McClendon, *Doctrine*, 417–52.

intentionally places the chapter "The Mission of the Church(es)" near the very beginning of his ecclesiology, following immediately the chapter "The Origin and Nature of the Church." It is, therefore, appropriate to explore first Garrett's mission theme before other ecclesial aspects. Garrett's church mission writings may be classified into three main sections: universal evangelism ("evangelization"), Christian unity ("ecumenism"), and social services ("ethics"). For Garrett, Christian mission is essentially related to the function of the universal priesthood of God's people, particularly to its aspects of universalization, obligation, and mediation of the gospel. Ecclesiology within the framework of the believers' priesthood stresses the *universality* of the gospel to all people at all times and the *obligation* of all Christians as *mediation* (or human agency) of the gospel to all people at all times by all means. This chapter specifically manifests a "Trinitarian" and a "discipleship" theme with respect to church mission.

Chapter 3 deals with another major subject in Garrett's ecclesiology, namely, the membership of the church in order to show that the teaching of believers' membership fundamentally correlates with the universal priesthood theme. A summary of Garrett's writings on church membership is divided into three subsections: "believers' church concept," "believer's baptism by immersion," and "born-again membership." The issue of church membership indispensably begins with the concept of the believers' church in Garrett's ecclesiology. A believers' church is composed of those who are regenerated by the Holy Spirit, of those who receive believers' baptism by immersion as an external confession of their internal reality, and of those who continue to commit to church discipline and discipleship. Garrett's emphasis on the "strict" or "closed" church membership is not a deviation but rather a correspondence to the priesthood of all believers, especially with regard to the aspects of regeneration-baptism, confession-commitment, and discipline-discipleship. It is evident in Garrett's writings that the final goal of accentuating the regenerate, committed, and disciplined church membership in ecclesiology is to make genuine disciples.

Chapter 4 argues that Garrett's view on the ministry of the church is directly founded on the priesthood of all believers, which is essentially patterned after Christ's high priestly person and work, mission and ministry. This section will find Garrett's direct explication and application of the teaching of the believers' priesthood to the general (lay) and special (ordained) ministries of the church. Based on his studies of the Old and New Testament priesthood, Garrett emphasizes the character and function of all Christians as God's ministers in participation of Christ's threefold priestly, prophetic, and kingly ministry, a ministry of servanthood. While Christ's priesthood is distinct from Christians' priesthood, the former is the pattern for the latter. Garrett suggests four priestly functions of the church in terms of "spiritual sacrifices": worship, witness, stewardship, and service. The ministry of the church is a direct consequence of the doctrine of the universal priesthood. Nevertheless, Garrett is concerned primarily with its corporate service (i.e., responsibility or obligation), although without denying its corollary for individual status (i.e., privilege) before God. This chapter will provide a succinct sketch of Garrett's views on the "priesthood of Christ," the "priesthood of Christians," and the "priesthood of the specially called" in order to demonstrate that Garrett's ministry of the church is rooted in the priesthood doctrine, especially with respect to communality-mutuality, universality-diversity, and equality-complementarity. The end of the church ministry is for the discipleship of the church, namely, to build up Christians as effective and faithful ministers or servants of Christ.

Chapter 5 attempts to show that the governance or management of the church is a direct application of Garrett's concept of the Christian priesthood. Garrett emphatically teaches that a particular congregation or a local church, rather than the civil state or government, has the *final* human authority to decide on all church issues, from membership to leadership to relationships; from ministration to administration to delegation; from doctrine to discipline to discipleship. Nonetheless, the *ultimate* authority of the church governance rests in the lordship of Christ (Christocracy) and the leadership of the Holy Spirit (pneumatophoria). While every member of a congregation has a voice or vote in all church decisions (democracy), no other external and superior authority, whether ecclesial or political, is to control or constrain the life of the particular congregation (autonomy). In this chapter, this writer will provide a summary of Garrett's perspectives on church management with respect to "church-state relations," "congregational polity," and "church discipline." The congregation has the final authority to decide on all matters of the church—in particular, church discipline, an aspect which has been much neglected and avoided—and to call for proper separation of authority between the church and the state. The believers' priesthood as specifically applied in congregational polity, church discipline, and church-state relations is to encourage accountable disciples of Christ through responsible authority, full participation, and communal discipleship.

In the final chapter, this writer will conclude that the priesthood of all believers is a unifying and guiding theme of Garrett's ecclesiology—mission, membership, ministry, and management—whether by its implication, function, derivation, correlation, foundation, or application. Nonetheless, the priesthood theme is not the *sole* governing motif in Garrett's ecclesiology. Garrett's concept of the church also lies within the Trinitarian and discipleship rubrics of ecclesiology, two complementary principles that help construct a biblically-balanced Baptist ecclesiology.

VALUE OF THE RESEARCH

Restore Unity, Recover Identity, and Refine Orthopraxy has significance for academics and churches alike. First, this book is to be the first monograph that attempts to discover, discern, and determine the central concerns or thoughts of a leading Southern Baptist thinker who has contributed widely-referenced writings in the discipline of Baptist theology, especially, Baptist ecclesiology and its distinctives.[16] Subsequent generations who intend to research Baptist ecclesiology will have to encounter Garrett's works on ecclesiology. To neglect his ecclesiological contributions to Baptist theology and life may be tantamount to rejecting a biblical and balanced ecclesiology. Second, Garrett's theological methodology, explicitly centralized in the doctrine of the universal priesthood, implicitly connected to the doctrine of the Trinity, and necessarily coalesced into the doctrine of discipleship, is a wholesome way of doing ecclesiology. The believers' priesthood connected with the Trinitarian and the discipleship motifs is an adequate theological principle that unifies various ecclesial themes and balances doctrine with practice. Third, the Christian priesthood motif, adequately expounded and appreciated, may also function to establish the identity and the boundary of the church. To discover who we are and who we are not, or to affirm what we believe and what we do not believe, may sound crude or rude, but ultimately leads to our theological distinctiveness without causing testy divisiveness.[17] Fourth, a renewed

---

16. Paul Basden contributed two biographical essays on Garrett's life and writings, but without scrutinizing Garrett's ecclesiology: Basden, "James Leo Garrett Jr.," 297–316; idem, "James Leo Garrett, Jr.," 132–47.

17. Dockery, "Southern Baptists in the Twenty-First Century," 18.

understanding of the doctrine of the royal priesthood is "potentially a powerful means for church renewal."[18] The biblical priesthood not only fosters the common fellowship or relationship among Christians but also challenges and motivates those who are yet to participate in this common priesthood to take initiative and become effective in church ministries.[19]

GARRETT'S REDISCOVERY AND REDEFINITION OF THE PRIESTHOOD OF ALL BELIEVERS

The doctrine of the universal priesthood was a major discovery and recovery in the sixteenth-century Reformation, in addition to the doctrines of justification by faith and *sola scriptura*. The priesthood doctrine has become a common heritage or property of all major Christian denominations today. Nevertheless, not all churches clearly grasp the fundamental meanings of the doctrine or its implications. Consequently, not all churches faithfully or consistently follow the notion of the universal priesthood.

Garrett's Biblical Exposition of the Universal Priesthood

The concept of the universal priesthood has become noticeable in Garrett's ecclesiology since the late 1950s. In his earlier writing, Garrett's evangelical explication of the traditional formula, the *extra ecclesiam nulla salus* ("outside the Church no salvation"), in terms of "outside Jesus Christ no salvation" already indicates his incipient concern for the intimate relationship between the church and the priesthood of all believers: those who truly believe in or belong to Christ are "members of the body of Christ," as in Paul's language (1 Cor 12:27); "a chosen race, a royal priesthood, a holy nation, God's own people," as in Peter's language (1 Pet 2:9); and "visible saints," as in the seventeenth-century English Baptists' language.[20] On the one hand, Garrett is emphatic that Christ, not the institutionalized church, is the one and only true mediator between God and sinners. On the other hand, Garrett virtually makes synonymous the concepts of "Christ's body," "royal priesthood," and "visible saints," all referring to the character and/or function of the church.

---

18. Garrett, *Systematic Theology*, 2:618.
19. Garrett, "Priesthood of All Believers," 4.
20. Garrett, "Outside the Church No Salvation," 7.

Garrett's conviction and commitment to the believers' priesthood became evident in the early 1960s when he penned "The Priesthood of All Believers" and "Recovering My Priesthood."[21] Garrett confesses that many Christians, including himself, often interpreted the royal priesthood in an individualistic manner, emphasizing individual privileges and authority; for example, direct access to God, the personal right to vote, and the individual ability to interpret Scripture; all of which are not the essential meaning of the biblical priesthood. It is true that all Christians fully and truly participate in the priesthood, but the Christian priesthood, as Garrett stresses, is not to be taken as a singular or individual "priest," nor to be applied to any particular Christian leadership, and never to be identified as a spiritual gift. For the apostles, the common Christian priesthood "was as wide as the early Christian *ekklesia*" and a matter of "the corporate Christian life, veritably a corollary of the doctrine of the church."[22] Without further ado, the following provides a succinct preview and review of Garrett's exploration of the Christian priesthood from biblical, historical, theological, and pastoral perspectives.

Biblically, there are New Testament passages teaching explicitly the priesthood of all Christians: 1 Peter 2:4–10; Revelation 1:5–6; 5:9–10; 20:6; Hebrews 13:15–19. The New Testament idea of Christian priesthood is undeniably rooted in the Old Testament concept of priesthood. Soon after the Israelites came out of Egypt and arrived at Mount Sinai, Moses went up to the mountain to receive God's word and will on behalf of the people. By God's sovereign act of deliverance, Israel was to become God's "own possession among all the peoples," "a kingdom of priests," and "a holy nation," contingent upon their voluntary obedience and faithfulness to God's covenant (Exod 19:4–6a).[23] In particular, the future tenses

---

21. Garrett, "The Priesthood of All Believers," 4. Idem, "Recovering My Priesthood," 14–15. See Smith, *Making of the 1963 Baptist Faith and Message.* Garrett pointed out to this present writer about Appendix 4 "A Declaration of Basic Beliefs" written by Garrett for the Southern Baptist Convention's Baptist Faith & Message Committee in the summer of 1962. The article on the church has no reference to the priesthood of all Christians. This indicates that the doctrine had not yet come to be of major significance in his ecclesiology.

22. Garrett, "Recovering My Priesthood," 14.

23. "You yourselves have seen what I did to the Egyptians, and *how* I bore you on eagles' wings, and brought you to Myself. Now then, if you will indeed obey My voice and keep My covenant, then you shall be My own possession among all the peoples, for all the earth is Mine; and you shall be to Me a kingdom of priests and a holy nation." All

of verses 5–6, "you shall be," point to the future realization of this declaration.[24] The term "a kingdom of priests" means "the priestly character and function of Israel under Yahweh's kingship, especially in relation to non-Israelite peoples."[25] Garrett perceives a gradual transition from the Aaronic or "prophetic" priesthood to the "peoplic" priesthood by emphasizing the sacrificial function; the latter became the primary assumption of the New Testament writers.[26]

The "Suffering Servant of the Lord" passages (Isa 42:1–4; 49:1–7; 50:4–9; 52:13—53:12; 61:6) contain the priesthood motif which provides an appropriate transition to the priesthood of Christ and of Christians. While the prophetic and kingly elements were ascribed to the "Servant,"[27] the sacrificial function of the "Servant" was more prominent: the Servant was rejected, suffered, and died willingly for the sins of others (Isa 53:3–12); the Servant's mission was universal, transcending the boundary of Israel (Isa 49:6). That Israel was to fulfill corporately the priestly function prefigured the coming High Priest, who in turn initiated the corporate priesthood of Christians.[28] The pattern of the Suffering Servant becomes the pattern of the priesthood of Christ; the pattern of the High Priest determines the pattern of the priesthood of all Christians.

Despite the fact that Jesus did not identify himself as a priest or think of himself in terms of priesthood, nor was he in the official priesthood, one cannot overlook, for instance, Jesus' sacrificially self-giving service (Mark 10:45; Luke 22:27); his so-called "High-priestly Prayer" (John 17); and his perfect, precious, and permanent High-priestly role (Heb 2:17; 4:15–16; 7:23–28; 9:9—10:18).[29] While Christ's priesthood is not identical with the Christian priesthood in the New Testament, the former is the foundational motif and model of the latter. The overall pattern behind

---

scriptural references are from the *New American Standard Bible* (1995), unless indicated otherwise.

24. Garrett, "Biblical Doctrine of the Priesthood," 138.
25. Ibid., 139.
26. Ibid., 141.
27. Depending on its contexts, the "Servant" may be interpreted as the individual (e.g., Isaiah, Jeremiah), as the idealized (i.e., the remnant of Israel), or as the collective (i.e., the entire people of Israel).
28. Garrett, "Biblical Doctrine of the Priesthood," 142.
29. Ibid., 144–45.

Jesus' ministry is his self-sacrificial service and servanthood on behalf of other people.

First Peter 2:4–10 explicitly teaches that all Christians are priests. Borrowing the terms from Exodus 19:5–6, Peter identified the Christians as "a holy priesthood" (1 Pet 2:5), "a chosen race, a royal priesthood, a holy nation, God's own people" (1 Pet 2:9a). John asserted that Christ by his sacrificial blood "made us to be a kingdom, priests to his God and Father" (Rev 1:6a) and made the redeemed from various nations "*to be* a kingdom and priests to our God; and they will reign upon the earth" (Rev 5:10). In the future, the resurrected Christians will be "priests of God and of Christ and will reign with Him for a thousand years" (Rev 20:6). Garrett stresses that all these texts use either "priesthood" or "priests" in the plural, never in the singular "priest." In addition, the term "priest" appears neither on the lists of "spiritual gifts" (Rom 12:4–8; 1 Cor 12:4–11, 27–31; Eph 4:7–14; 1 Pet 4:10–11), nor on the lists for church leadership qualifications (1 Tim 3:1–13; Titus 1:5–9); therefore, the priesthood belongs not to certain people, but to all Christians, to the Christian community. The New Testament teaches a communal character of the Christian priesthood, not a special or clerical priesthood.[30]

Garrett's Historical Development of the Doctrine

Historically, Garrett investigates the views on the priesthood of Christians of the early churches, i.e., of the pre-Cyprianic and post-Cyprianic periods. The early church fathers did not deal either extensively or exclusively with the doctrine of the universal priesthood, but the theme of "spiritual sacrifices" is perceivable.[31] Tertullian was the pioneer who explicitly placed the ordained clergy in the special "sacerdotal" category, while at

---

30. Ibid., 146–47.

31. Of the writings of the Apostolic Fathers, only the *Didache*, Clement, Ignatius, and Polycarp mentioned about Christians' offering of "spiritual sacrifices"; the first two refer to sacrifices of worship, the latter two to the sacrifice of martyrdom. Irenaeus of Lyons primarily identified priestly sacrifices with the Eucharist. Clement of Alexandria tended to restrict the general priesthood to the "pneumatics," who were alone qualified to offer spiritual sacrifices of themselves, praises, prayers, and Scripture reading. While emphasizing Christ's priestly work, Origen distinguished special priesthood from general priesthood. The former refers to the apostles, the scholars, and the martyrs; the latter to all Christians offering spiritual sacrifices of praise, prayers, holiness, purity, righteousness, and pity. Garrett, "Pre-Cyprianic Doctrine of the Priesthood of all Christians," 47, 50, 52, 54, 57, 58.

the same time affirming the universal priesthood of believers.[32] Although the doctrine of the universal priesthood of believers was not completely eclipsed in the early church fathers, its biblical meaning was restricted, or modified at the least, to fit the exigency of the church, especially at the time of Cyprian.

Cyprian unambiguously and exclusively applied the term "priests" to the ordained clergy, especially the bishops. Nowhere did he teach specifically the priesthood of all believers, nor quote the clear passages on the universal priesthood, although he did retain prayers and merciful deeds as spiritual sacrifices to God.[33] Cyprian's accentuation of the special clerical priesthood seemed to become influential and prevalent in both the fourth-century Greek East and Latin West, in which the theme of "spiritual sacrifices" was generally retained and the "universal priesthood" was basically unappreciated. Nevertheless, Garrett detects the acknowledgment of the royal priesthood of all Christians by Gregory of Nazianzus, Ambrose of Milan, and Augustine of Hippo, who made particular reference to 1 Peter 2:5, 9 and Revelation 20:6.[34]

Luther was one of the very first Reformers who recovered the doctrine of the priesthood of all believers. Luther used the concept to undermine the "Romanist" idea that the spiritual power above is superior to the temporal power; to deny the teaching of the mass and defend spiritual sacrifices; to attack the idea of ordination as a sacrament; and also to argue for the biblical mandate for lay Christians to teach, especially when there was no Christian teacher. Regardless of the exact significance of the royal priesthood doctrine in John Calvin and Peter Martyr Vermigli (1499–1562), Garrett perceives that both emphasized the offering of spiritual "sacrifices" in the form of thanksgiving, prayer, praise, and service in fulfillment of the priesthood of all Christians.[35]

The Protestants in later centuries applied and expressed the doctrine of the Christian priesthood in their unique ways. Garrett summarized concisely:

> Later Protestant denominations tended not so much to teach the central truth of the universal priesthood as to apply it in vari-

---

32. Ibid., 60.
33. Garrett, "Priesthood of All Christians," 22–23.
34. Garrett, *Systematic Theology*, 2:612.
35. Ibid., 2:612–13.

ous ways. The Church of England restored the cup in the Lord's Supper to the laity and produced the English Bible and the Book of Common Prayer. For Puritans the universal priesthood provided the basis for church reform, for Separatists/Congregationalists it led to congregational polity and the church meeting, for Baptists it was expressed in believer's baptism and religious liberty, and for Quakers it meant Spirit-led worship, the Inner Light, and the absence of pastoral ministry. Anglican Evangelicals stressed preaching of the gospel, congregational singing of psalms and hymns, and societal reform, and Wesleyan Methodism found apostolic succession unnecessary, formed bands and classes, and utilized lay preachers.[36]

In summary, the doctrine of the priesthood of all Christians was partially *retained* by the early church fathers, clearly *restricted* by Cyprian, virtually *repressed* in the Middle Ages, definitely *rediscovered* by the early Reformers, consequently *reinterpreted* by later Protestants, and eventually *restored*, at least in Garrett's attempt, to its rightful place in ecclesiology.

The Theological Significance of the Christian Priesthood

Theologically, Garrett notes the essential significance of the believers' priesthood. First, the doctrine of the universal priesthood is based on, though not identical with, the person and work of the High Priest, Jesus Christ, who is the only perfect and effective mediator opening once and for all the access for sinners to God and who also becomes the fundamental pattern for the church and its ministry.[37] The notion of "direct access" to God's presence belongs primarily and rightfully to Christ the High Priest alone (Heb 4:14–16), not to the common Christian priesthood.[38] Christians are not to offer propitiatory or expiatory sacrifices, the works Christ has accomplished perfectly and effectively, but are to follow the pattern Christ the High Priest has set for church, i.e., the prophetic,

---

36. Ibid., 2:613–14.

37. Ibid., 2:603.

38. Garrett's quest for the common priesthood initially grew out of his dissatisfaction with and rejection of the "direct access" view which overemphasized individual privilege, right, or capability to approach God. Garrett does not deny the fact about Christian's free access to the Father based on Christ's priesthood, as taught in Heb 4:14–16, but he rejects the teaching that the "direct access" is derivative of the universal priesthood. See Barry Garrett, "Priesthood of Believers," 1113–14; and Pinson, "Baptists."

priestly, and princely servanthood (*diakonia*).[39] The biblical priesthood of all believers accentuates its service, rather than its status.[40]

Second, one enters the royal priesthood by no other way than by becoming a Christian, i.e., voluntary repentance and faith in Christ.[41] The regenerate experience as symbolized in believer's baptism and ratified with church membership is requisite for participating in offering "spiritual sacrifices," i.e., participating in various priestly ministries.[42] The universal priesthood properly and biblically belongs not to all people universally, but to Christians only who by believing in Christ participate in his priestly ministry.[43] Garrett acknowledges that no explicit connection exists between baptism and the royal priesthood in the New Testament, and no biblical evidence suggests that baptism is ordination into the universal priesthood, but there exists a logical and theological correspondence between the admission to church and the admission to the priesthood through faith in Christ alone as signified by baptism.[44] Luther also stated, "Through baptism all of us are consecrated to the [royal or common] priesthood."[45] Although baptism does not belong to the most basic meaning of the Christian priesthood, belief in Christ affirmed in water baptism is a necessary and essential step into the common priesthood for spiritual sacrifices.

Third, the royal priesthood emphasizes essentially its corporate aspect of believers, without jettisoning its implications or applications to individual Christians. Garrett finds that the primary meaning of the Christian priesthood must have some corporate or communal significance. The universal priesthood does not mean that a Christian is his own priest, but all Christians are priests to each other (believers) and to others (non-believers). The former indicates communality of saints in corporate worship, fellowship, and prayers, whereas the latter suggests

---

39. Garrett, "Biblical Doctrine of the Priesthood," 142–43, 146.
40. George, "Priesthood of All Believers," 92.
41. Garrett, "Priesthood of All Believers," 4.
42. Yarnell, "Congregational Priesthood," 123.
43. George, "Priesthood of All Believers," 86. Evidently, Garrett's "Christian priesthood" parts with E. Y. Mullins's "soul competency" (i.e., the latter belongs to all human beings). See Yarnell, "Congregational Priesthood," 123.
44. Garrett, *Systematic Theology*, 2:610; Yarnell, "Priesthood of Believers," 240.
45. Luther, *Open Letter to the Christian Nobility*.

accountability of all Christians for evangelization, proclamation, or witnessing.[46] The communal understanding of the priesthood doctrine, however, comprises its applications to individual Christians: each Christian's obligation to be involved in, for example, intercessory prayer and Bible study, whether in private or in group. The personalized understanding of the royal priesthood, namely, a Christian's ability to interpret the Bible under the Spirit's guidance, the privilege to vote in church matters, or the congregation's polity, is not its primary meaning in the Bible, but the derivatives or implications of the common priesthood.[47] Garrett is careful to be concerned with the primary meaning of the priesthood doctrine before coming to its implications or applications to individual Christians.

Fourth, the universal priesthood is the basis of general or lay ministry, but without being contradistinctive to the special or ordained ministry.[48] The New Testament never used the term "priest" as a spiritual gift or an office of church leadership; the term was never applied to certain individuals, but to all Christians.[49] Nevertheless, the specially called, the ordained ministries or offices are not contrary to, but derivative from the common priesthood. Garrett observes, "For Luther the called, ordained ministry is both derivative from the priesthood of all Christians and something directly instituted by Jesus Christ, and the call is both inner (from God) and outer (through men)."[50]

Practically, the crucial question is how Christians are to function as "priests" today. Garrett is convinced that the priesthood of all believers is "actually or potentially significant and applicable to the twentieth-century [or contemporary] scene."[51] The main and primary task of a Christian community as "priests" is to offer "spiritual sacrifices" to God on behalf of others. Garrett suggests some specific, though not exclusive, examples of "spiritual sacrifices," such as, worship, witness, stewardship, and service.[52] This specific list of "spiritual sacrifices" is not intended to

---

46. George, "Priesthood of All Believers," 92; Garrett, ed., *We Baptists*, 29.

47. Garrett, "Priesthood of All Believers," 4. Idem, "Recovering My Priesthood," 14.

48. Garrett, *Systematic Theology*, 2:604–37.

49. Ibid., 2:609.

50. Ibid., 2:624.

51. Garrett, "Biblical Doctrine of the Priesthood," 137.

52. Ibid., 148. "Spiritual sacrifices": First, Christians are to offer spiritual worship with their "fruit of lips" acknowledging Christ's name (Heb 13:15), with their whole "bodies" (Rom 12:1), with their purified "conscience" (Heb 9:14), with their repentant

be comprehensive, but a stepping-stone for an appropriate appreciation and application of the Christian priesthood in the fabric and rubric of universal evangelization, communal fellowship, mutual servanthood, and congregational participation.

The doctrine of the universal priesthood is particularly and pastorally applied to congregational polity; namely, a local church as a royal priesthood is to participate in the decision-making of the congregation.[53] The priesthood doctrine understood in terms of corporate responsibility and communal servanthood necessarily implies the participation of the whole local Christian congregation in discerning and determining God's will for the church under the lordship of Christ and leadership of the Spirit. Collectively, the whole church has the final authority to decide on all matters with respect to membership, ordination, worship, doctrines, and discipline. Individually, every church member has the responsibility to voice or vote with regard to all those matters. Garrett concludes that church polity is "not an end but only a means to other ends—growth and maturity of Christians unto Christ-likeness, the proclamation of the gospel to all nations and peoples, and the coming of the kingdom of God 'on earth as it is in heaven.'"[54] To function as a common priesthood, the local church is to fulfill the roles of responsible and corporate ministration, participation, proclamation, and discipleship.

On the one hand, it would be an overstatement that Garrett has exhausted the meanings and implications of the doctrine of the universal priesthood. On the other hand, it would be an understatement that the doctrine is not integral to his ecclesiology. Despite being abused and misused throughout history in the hands of many a theologian, the royal priesthood is, nonetheless, a biblical doctrine clearly stated and taught in Scripture. Garrett consistently returns to the doctrine to explore, explicate, and express its essential meanings and implications pertinent to ecclesiology. This preliminary review suggests that Garrett's doctrine of

---

hearts (Ps 51:16–17), and with their intercessory prayers (Heb 13:18–19). Second, the priesthood of Christians involves witness or evangelization (Rom 15:15–16), that is, to declare or proclaim God's salvific work in Christ (1 Pet 2:10). Third, Christian stewardship, for example, in monetary giving with steadfast faith, is a pleasing sacrifice to God (Phil 4:18). Fourth, the priestly sacrifice of Christians include service (*diakonia*), as in bearing and sharing with fellow Christians or doing benevolent works (Heb 13:16).

53. Garrett, "Congregation-Led Church: Congregational Polity," 185.
54. Garrett, *Systematic Theology*, 2:645.

the universal priesthood impinges upon some major aspects of his ecclesiology, specifically, the mission, membership, ministry, and management of the church.

CONCLUSION

After reviewing Garrett's view on the believers' priesthood, this present writer will immediately begin to delve into Garrett's ecclesiology to argue that Garrett's major ecclesial writings on "mission," "membership," "ministry," and "management" consistently manifest the Christian priesthood theme. Universal Gospel mission, regenerate church membership, corporate Christian ministry, and congregational church management point distinctly and distinctively to the nature and function of the priesthood of all believers. Nonetheless, as will be observed periodically from the chapters, this present writer shows that the distinct works of the three persons of the Godhead play an important, though implicit, role in Garrett's development and construction of ecclesiology. Furthermore, all of Garrett's ecclesial themes eventually converge on the pastoral motif of discipline-discipleship, a vital element that Garrett has been eager to recover and restore to its rightful and biblical status. Stated concisely, the following chapters will demonstrate and illustrate that Garrett's doctrine of the church is *explicitly* based on the universal priesthood motif, while *implicitly* rooted in a Trinitarian motif and *intrinsically* applied to the discipleship motif.

chapter 2

The Mission of the Church

INTRODUCTION

THE PURPOSE OF THIS chapter is to demonstrate that Garrett's mission theme, while frequently manifesting Trinitarian and discipleship aspects, consistently revolves around the character and function of the believers' priesthood in respect to universalization, mediation, and obligation. The first main section provides a selective and, to a certain extent, interpretive review of Garrett's pertinent works on the mission of the church, pertaining to the aspects of "evangelization," "ecumenism," and "ethics." The second main section is an attempt to give an analytical evaluation of Garrett's view on church mission by means of interaction with other contemporary or recent theologians, particularly Herschel H. Hobbs, Robert A. Muthiah, and Lesslie Newbigin.

EVANGELIZATION: UNIVERSAL EVANGELISM

In "Authority for the Christian World Mission," Garrett holds that the authority of the church mission—the right to rule and power to do—is founded on the triune God.[1] The *purpose* of the Father was to create, choose, and call forth a distinct people, a kingdom, or a nation of priests (Exod 19:6)—a distinctive group that will eventually embrace people from every nation or language worthy of worship of the triune God (Rev 4:11; 5:8–9). The Father sent his Son to fulfill this very mission by the

---

1. Garrett, "Authority for the Christian World Mission," 74–76.

propitiation of the Son, the one and only provision of redemption (Rom 3:25–26; 1 John 2:2). The Son's mission, centered in the cross (i.e., crucifixion and resurrection), is the foundation of the Great Commission. "As the Father has sent me, I also send you," Jesus explained to his disciples (John 20:21b). The *powerful presence* of the Holy Spirit is the legitimacy of and the dynamic for the church mission (John 15:26; Acts 1:8). Concisely, the mission of the Trinity is the ground of Christian universal mission.

The church mission of making disciples involves extending the gospel to all people (Matt 28:19), at all times (Matt 28:20), and by all means (1 Cor 9:22).[2] All Christians, as agents or instruments of the triune God, are obliged to fulfill the Great Commission because they belong to God's distinct people, the royal priesthood (1 Pet 2:9–10).[3] In light of this Christian priesthood, Garrett is convinced that every Christian, ordained or otherwise, is to participate in the gospel witness. Every Christian is a "missionary." The church, as the people of God, exists by mission and for mission. To be the true *ecclesia* of Christ is to engage in universal evangelization, a ministry which is opened to the whole "laity" (Greek *laos* in 1 Peter 2:10 means "people") as well as the clergy. This "unrealized potential of the witness of professing Christians" is the hope of the modern reformation.[4]

Garrett further explores a theology of church mission/evangelism in relation to Christian discipleship. In *Evangelism for Discipleship*, the Baptist theologian uses his own modified version of *ordo salutis* as an attempt to unify God's grace of salvation (orthodoxy) and Christian obligation in disciplined discipleship (orthopraxy).[5] A beginning of new life requires the works of the Trinity and the responses of a person in repentance and faith. Hence, the believing person is begotten of God the Father, recreated in Christ, and regenerated by the Spirit.[6] The assurance of the new life rests in the evidence of discipleship, which involves learning, disciplining, cross-bearing, and evangelizing, both individually and

2. Ibid., 77–79.

3. Ibid., 80–82.

4. Ibid., 82.

5. Garrett, *Evangelism for Discipleship*, 5. Garrett states that the basic reason for replacing "justification" and "faith" with the themes "new life" and "discipleship" is "to bring together the gracious gift of God's grace and the duty of disciplined Christian discipleship."

6. Ibid., 37, 44.

corporately.⁷ Garrett's particular attention to the practical implications of every expounded doctrine, especially of discipleship, is obvious.⁸ As already manifest in the title *Evangelism for Discipleship*, Garrett drives home the central teaching that making disciples is the aim of Christian mission entrusted to all who belong to the universal priesthood of believers (1 Pet 2:9–10).⁹ Succinctly, to be God's royal priesthood is to make disciples so that they may be Christlike ("holy" or "sanctified"). The process and end of discipleship ultimately are the work of the Trinity.¹⁰ In concluding his exposition, Garrett intentionally applies the theology of mission for discipleship to an issue of Christian unity (Heb 12:14).¹¹ The mission of the church, the evangelism for discipleship, or the call to Christlikeness must involve the unity of Christian churches.

The chapter on "Mission of the Church(es)" in Garrett's *Systematic Theology* explores the "universalist" elements in the Bible. The Trinitarian aspect is still detectable, though not distinctly evident in the chapter. God's original and ultimate purpose as revealed in the Old Testament was to include all nations through the nation of Israel (Exod 19:5–6; Isa 42:6–7; 49:6).¹² Christ's words and works—especially his death, resurrection, and Great Commission—were for both Jews and Gentiles (Mark 10:45; 1 John 2:2; 1 Cor 15:22; Matt 28:18–20).¹³ The coming of the Spirit at Pentecost contained "universal symbolism, spiritual empowerment, and eschatological significance" (Acts 1–2).¹⁴ By his total dependence on the Holy Spirit, Paul preached the gospel and reached the Gentiles.¹⁵ Garrett concludes the biblical section on universal mission by pointing out the Petrine priesthood passage (1 Pet 2:9–12) to emphasize that Christians as God's "chosen people" readily proclaimed Christ verbally and exemplarily

---

7. Ibid., 37, 48, 51–60.

8. Practical implications include the ethical fruit of repentance (ibid., 15–18), the applications of forgiveness (26–29), the ministry of reconciliation (32–34), the fruitage of new life (47–48), the implications of discipleship (51–60), and the relevance of sanctification (67, 72–74).

9. Ibid., 58.

10. Ibid., 68–69.

11. Ibid., 73–74.

12. Garrett, *Systematic Theology*, 2:527–31.

13. Ibid., 2:532–37.

14. Ibid., 2:538.

15. Ibid., 2:539–41.

to all peoples.¹⁶ In dealing with the historical development of the church mission, Garrett explains that all churches and Christians, whether ordained or lay, were agents of evangelization, as was probably the case in the earliest Christian centuries. As he concludes the chapter on "Mission of the Church(es)," Garrett raises some contemporary issues on church mission, without offering any significant theological conclusions on the subject. Nonetheless, the concepts of the universality of the mission, the obligation of all Christians to carry out the Great Commission, and the human mediation of the gospel are conspicuous throughout the chapter.¹⁷

ECUMENISM: CHRISTIAN UNITY

The mission of the church, in Garrett's ecclesiological framework, necessarily entails the unity of Christian churches, i.e., Christian ecumenism. This writer has decided to collate Garrett's many pertinent writings on Christian unity into five succinct aspects: purport, people, postures, points, and purposes.

The *purport* of "ecumenism" that Garrett emphasizes is basically not a unity of world religions but of the Christian church.¹⁸ The term "church" here in respect to unity is not primarily used to refer to the eschatological or heavenly church, nor to every local or particular Christian congregation, but to all "visible" churches, i.e., "Christendom."¹⁹ Garrett explains that although the term ἐκκλησια (*ecclesia*) in the New Testament is mainly used in a local sense, there are undeniably some passages that employ a wider definition of the term (Eph 1:22; 3:10; 3:21; 5:23–32; Col 1:18, 24; 1 Cor 12:28), that is, ἐκκλησια as the "spiritual body of Christ."²⁰ While recognizing the divergent types, models, means, and foci in the pursuit of church unity,²¹ Garrett's main concern is not so

---

16. Ibid., 2:541.

17. Ibid., 2:527–48.

18. Garrett explains, "'Ecumenical' is derived from the Greek *oikoumenē*, 'the whole inhabited earth'" (see e.g., Matt 24:14; Luke 2:1; Acts 11:28; Rom 10:18; Heb 1:6; 2:5; Rev 3:10); Garrett, *Systematic Theology*, 2:520, footnote 103; see also 2:680–87. There is no indication that Garrett has ever written on "religious ecumenism" or has participated in "interfaith dialogues." Garrett also recognizes that the word "ecumenical" in the Bible is never associated explicitly with the church (Garrett, "Ecclesiology: The Crucial Issue," 6).

19. Garrett, *Systematic Theology*, 2:677.

20. Garrett, "Ecclesiology," October 14, 1954, 6; October 21, 1954, 8.

21. Garrett, "Problems, Issues, and Challenges in Christian Unity," 201–7.

much with the "organic," "institutional," or "organizational" as with the "spiritual" unity of Christian churches, a unity that may be "marked by love, may stress purity of doctrine and of lifestyle, and may be possible without organizational oneness."[22] Such unity involves both relational and doctrinal aspects.[23] On the other hand, in general agreement with Estep's and Erickson's reasons for nonmembership or nonparticipation in the World Council of Churches,[24] Garrett is concerned with the council's tendencies to undermine the authority of the Bible and to challenge Baptist distinctives by enforcing creeds; to threaten the autonomy of local churches by centralizing authority in one general body; to weaken universal evangelization by prioritizing political, economic, or social issues; and to move toward "a worldwide superchurch structure" despite its disclaimer.[25] He states concisely and realistically that church unity "begins at the congregational level, should never evoke satisfaction until it reaches out to Christians of all nations, and will never be fully realized until it is realized eschatologically."[26]

The *people* who have been in Garrett's main unifying work are of Roman Catholic, evangelical, free, and/or believers' churches. His earlier and consistent unifying effort focused on understanding Catholic theology and interacting with its theologians from Protestant or the Southern Baptist vantage points,[27] while continuously rediscovering his Southern

---

22. Garrett, *Systematic Theology*, 2:685. Structural or organizational oneness, such as that in the Roman Catholic Church, does not necessarily imply unity. Garrett points out that there are theological variations among Dominicans, Franciscans, and Jesuits, for example. In addition, there are "different levels or grades of certainty in Roman Catholic dogmatics" that may create complexity and difficulty in doctrinal unity. See Garrett, "Basic Theological Differences," 28–30.

23. Garrett, *Systematic Theology*, 1:147–51; 2:679–80, 685–87.

24. Estep, *Baptists and Christian Unity*, 168–88; Erickson, *Christian Theology*, 1148–51.

25. Garrett, *Systematic Theology*, 2:685. See also Garrett, "Ecclesiology," October 14,1954, 6–7; October 21, 1954, 8.

26. Garrett, *Systematic Theology*, 2:687.

27. Notably, Garrett, "Thomas Aquinas' Doctrine of Penance" (1949); idem, "Protestant Writings on Roman Catholicism" (1966); idem, "Shifting Foci of the Protestant-Roman Catholic Confrontation," 29–41; idem, *Reinhold Niebuhr on Roman Catholicism* (1972); idem, "John A. Mackay on the Roman Catholic Church," 111–28; idem, "Theology and Practice of Baptism," 65–72. This particular issue (Spring 1986, vol. 28, no. 2), edited by Garrett, contains more than twenty papers presented at the second triennium of the dialogue (1982–1984) between Southern Baptist and Roman Catholic

Baptist identity vis-à-vis other evangelical and Baptist groupings.[28] His roles as an official guest of the Secretariat for Promoting Christian Unity for the final week of the Second Vatican Council (1965),[29] as the organizing chairman of the first Conference on the Concept of the Believers' Church (1967), as the first chairman of the Study Commission on Cooperative Christianity (1968–1975),[30] and later, as the co-chairman of the Study and Research Division (1996–2000)[31] of the Baptist World Alliance (BWA) are indicative of his active involvement in promoting Christian unity among the various Christian denominations.[32]

The *postures* of the unity endeavor, according to Garrett, should essentially include all critical, conversional, and conversational dimensions.[33] In a historical survey of Baptists' dealings with Roman Catholics, Garrett is persuaded that Christian churches, especially those of his own Southern Baptist denomination, should continue to engage in polemical confrontation, universal evangelization, and fraternal discussion.[34] They have to remain constructively critical because there are real and basic doctrinal differences that are to be "honestly faced, rightly interpreted, and properly assessed."[35] They also are to engage in active witness or conversion because membership in any church, whether Roman Catholic or Baptist or other evangelical denomination, does not guarantee that one is a Christian or has final salvation.[36] While called to universal

---

scholars, revolving around the theme of grace.

28. In chronological order, particularly, Garrett, "Vital Issues for Southern Baptists" (1952), 2; idem, "Theology of Walter Thomas Conner" (1954); idem, "Vital Issues for Southern Baptists: 1968," 24–27; Garrett et al., *Are Southern Baptists 'Evangelicals'?* (1983), 31–127; Garrett, "Southern Baptists as Evangelicals" (1983), 10–20; idem, "Who Are Southern Baptists in 1989?" 12; idem, "Are Southern Baptists 'Evangelicals'? A Further Reflection" (1993), 218–23; idem, "Distinctive Identity of Southern Baptists vis-à-vis Other Baptists" (1996), 6–16; idem, "Southern Baptists, Evangelicals, and Southwestern" (2002), 6–9; idem, *Baptist Theology: A Four-Century Study* (2009).

29. Manley, *Baptist World Alliance*, 40; footnote 52.

30. A significant contribution of his leadership is the publication of Garrett, ed., *Baptist Relations with Other Christians* (1974).

31. A notable result is the publication of Garrett, ed., *We Baptists* (1999), a cooperative restatement of Baptist identity.

32. Garrett, "Baptist Identity and Christian Unity," 56.

33. Garrett, "Polemic, Conversion, and/or Dialogue," 340–42.

34. Garrett, *Baptists and Roman Catholicism*, 42–45.

35. Garrett, "Polemic, Conversion, and/or Dialogue," 340.

36. Ibid., 341. Garrett argues pointedly, "No Baptist says that every member of the

evangelization, churches are to be involved in dialogue or conversation. Garrett detects the reluctance, suspicion, or even hostility of the Southern Baptists toward dialogue with the Roman Catholic Church in particular, but he is hopeful for "the effectual outreach of the Christian mission to all men in this secularistic, fear-driven age in which Christians must truly be 'the light of the world.'"[37]

The *points* around which Garrett's unity endeavor revolves are the essential Christian doctrines (e.g., Trinity, Christ, Scripture, sin, grace, and/or evangelization) as points of agreement with other Christians, particularly evangelical groupings. The themes of ecclesiology (e.g., believer's baptism by immersion, regenerate membership, church discipline, separation of church and state, and/or world evangelism) are points at which he regards Baptist doctrines to be distinctive from other Christians.[38] For instance, Garrett argues affirmatively with a historical-theological approach to discover and identify the commonalities of Southern Baptists and the evangelicals. Garrett concludes that "*Southern Baptists are denominational Evangelicals. They belong to and exemplify the great heritage of Scriptural authority, Christocentric doctrine, gospel proclamation, experience of Grace, and evangelical endeavor which is Evangelicalism.*"[39] On the one hand, Garrett attempts to understand fairly other Christians' convictions and identify common grounds of faith in order to foster Christian harmony.[40] On the other hand, he faithfully pres-

---

Roman Catholic Church is a Christian . . . Few Baptists, if any, would deny absolutely that any member of the Roman Catholic Church can possibly be a Christian. Those who hold that membership in a Baptist or other evangelical church does not *per se* guarantee that one is a Christian can hardly afford to deny that the saving grace of God may be operative in the life of one who is nevertheless a member of a religious structure that corrupts and hinders the free access of the gracious God to sinful men through Jesus Christ."

37. Ibid., 342.

38. Garrett, "Major Emphases in Baptist Theology," 36–46.

39. Garrett et al., *Are Southern Baptists 'Evangelicals'?*, 126. Italics original. See also Garrett, "Southern Baptists as Evangelicals," 10–20; idem, "Are Southern Baptists 'Evangelicals'? A Further Reflection," 218–23. It is interesting to note that the theme of "universal evangelization," contingent upon contexts, is a point of agreement or difference in Garrett's writings on Christian unity.

40. Garrett, *Baptist Theology*, 1–5. Garrett opens his survey by identifying common doctrines among the Roman Catholic, Eastern Orthodox, and Protestant churches. Baptists in general affirm, explicitly or implicitly, the Nicene (AD 325), Constantinopolitan (AD 381), Chalcedon (AD 451) confessional statements of Christ's two full natures united in one person, the Holy Spirit's full deity, and hence, the Trinity.

ents and represents Southern Baptists' convictions to other Christians without compromising his Baptist distinctives.[41] Moreover, Garrett is not timid about confronting the points of disagreement with, for example, the Roman Catholics concerning the meaning of sacraments, the role of the Virgin Mary, and the Petrine office.[42]

The theological *purposes* behind Garrett's seemingly indefatigable efforts toward Christian unity may be reduced to three interconnected themes: the oneness of the Trinity, the ministry of reconciliation, and the commission of discipleship. In his exposition of the high-priestly prayer of Jesus (John 17), Garrett preached on the oneness of the Trinity as the foundation of the unity of the churches.[43] Unity is, first of all, not grounded in human work but in divine will. Thus, all Christian churches, despite differences and distinctives, are God's people called as agents to carry out the ministry of reconciliation, which has been accomplished and initiated by Christ in his priestly office. Reconciliation must include not only the divine-human dimension, but also the human-human dimension, whereas the latter has been frequently neglected in Reformed and Baptist writings.[44] Garrett says pointedly, "Reconciliation on the ethical level must issue from reconciliation on the doctrinal level. 2 Corinthians 5 and Romans 5 must be joined with Ephesians 2 and Colossians 1 . . . [T]hose reconciled by God to God are commanded and expected to be reconciled to other human beings."[45] In other words, all Christians are agents of reconciliation in order to fulfill the Great Commission of

---

The superiority of Scripture, universality of sin, and necessity of grace, as doctrines of the early church, are also generally held by Baptists.

41. Garrett, "Baptist 'Distinctives': Endangered Species." In this sermon, Garrett identifies three Baptist distinctives: believer's baptism by immersion, religious freedom for all humans, and cooperative missions. See also idem, "Distinctive Identity of Southern Baptists vis-à-vis Other Baptists," 6–16.

42. Garrett, "Shifting Foci," 29–41. According to Garrett, at the Vatican in 2000, Walter Cardinal Kasper, leader in Pontifical Council for Promoting Christian Unity, commented on this article and suggested its use as a guide for later regional dialogues. As it was told to Garrett, in Buenos Aires of 2001, the participants used the article for dialogic purpose.

43. Garrett, "Chapel: April 11, 1997." That Garrett preached on Christian unity based on his exposition of John 17 as his last chapel message before his retirement from his professorship at Southwestern Baptist Seminary indicates his lifelong concern for the unity of all Christians.

44. Garrett, "Christian Doctrine of Reconciliation," 1–4, 25–29.

45. Ibid., 28.

discipleship. By studying the official documents of Vatican Council II, Garrett rightly emphasizes the missionary role of all God's people, both clergy and laypeople. He writes, "All baptized persons 'are consecrated in a spiritual house and a holy priesthood,' and 'everywhere on earth they must bear witness to Christ.'" All God's people participate in Christ's priestly, prophetic, and royal office and, therefore, are to fulfill the universal mission as God's priesthood.[46]

ETHICS: SOCIAL SERVICES

Garrett's works and writings on church unity inevitably lead to the issue of ethical effort or social service as an essential part of the mission of the church. Although he does not specifically articulate a theology of ethics,[47] it is not difficult to notice that Garrett's works on church unity frequently end with the call for impacting the society in general. For instance, in his address to a group of Baptist missionaries, Garrett unambiguously called for a strategy that "conceivably could combine missionary apologetics and evangelistic methods to be used by Evangelicals, theological and ethical interchange between Evangelicals and Roman Catholics, and areas of active cooperation between Evangelicals and Roman Catholics," a cooperation in the name of Jesus Christ that involves, for example, common Bible ministries to produce a Protestant-Roman Catholic Bible in various languages for different people, common medical ministries to benefit the sick in the remote communities, common teaching ministries to help the illiterate read and write, and common social ministries to alleviate poverty and deprivation by "strengthening social and economic reforms," without, however, sacrificing one's doctrinal and practical convictions.[48] Garrett states,

> If we share in the mission of Him who was sent by the Father and would be His witnesses to all mankind, we should be indifferent neither to what He is doing among all who confess him as Lord and Son of God nor to His purpose to unite all who believe in Him

---

46. Garrett, "Roman Catholicism and Baptist Missions," 2–3.

47. Garrett admits the influence by T. B. Maston, former professor of ethics at Southwestern Baptist Seminary, trained at Yale University. See Garrett, "Baptist Identity and Christian Unity," 55.

48. Garrett, "Roman Catholicism and Baptist Missions," 10.

"that the world may believe" that the Father has sent Him and has loved them (John 17:21, 23).[49]

The aspects of evangelizing effort, ecclesial unity, and ethical works are intertwined in Garrett's concept of church mission.

For Garrett, church mission in Christian evangelization and social involvement is not an either/or, but a both/and approach.[50] The biblical foundation for Garrett's approach is God's electing and loving purpose, particularly God's choosing Israel to bring the gospel to all nations (Deut 7:6–10; Isa 49:5). This universal task involved not only calling for the people to turn from idolatry and to turn toward Yahweh, but also addressed the "exploitation of the poor, dishonesty in business practices, and selfish luxury." The divine-promised and Spirit-anointed Servant was to establish justice in all nations without violence, as well as to bring the gospel to the people, especially the oppressed and the depressed (Isa 42:1–4; 60:1–3).[51]

The mission of Christ is the foundation for the mission of God's new people, the church. Garrett states, "The apostles interpreted their own role and the mission of the post-Pentecostal *ecclesia* as derivative from and expressive of the salvific or reconciling work of the crucified and risen Messiah and Lord." Paul declared that the gospel is the power of God in Christ that created a new people from Jews and Gentiles, a people that was given the ministry of reconciliation based on the reconciling work of Christ (Rom 1:16; 2 Cor 5:17–20). Peter also urged the people of God as "a royal priesthood" to declare the salvific work of Christ and to do good works that would bring nations to Christ (1 Pet 2:9, 12). Garrett states, "According to both Peter and Paul the work of Christ has a corporate dimension and has had distinct social effects."[52]

Garrett defines "evangelism" in the Trinitarian terms of "bearing witness" to the gospel of God revealed and fulfilled in the person and work of Christ Jesus, for the purpose of persuading and inviting people to respond in repentance and faith to the "regenerative work of God the Holy Spirit."[53] Regarding "social involvement," Garrett focuses on Christians' individual or corporate works in human society or "outside

---

49. Ibid.
50. Garrett, "Evangelism and Social Involvement," 60–62.
51. Ibid., 54.
52. Ibid., 54–55.
53. Ibid.

the church" for the public well-being. He further distinguishes the social effort under two aspects. First, *diakonal service*, as the "duty and privilege of Christians," is a Christian ministry of helping, caring, sharing, or healing to fellow Christians and general community. Second, through *social action*, Christians, whether individually or corporately, are to impact and reform the socioeconomic and political systems to promote the well-being of humanity in view of the divine purpose.[54]

Gospel proclamation and social services go hand in hand as the mission of the church. Garrett contends that the church that is truly built upon the "servanthood of its Lord" is to maintain the balance between the human-God reconciliation and human-human reconciliation: "Christians must engage both in proclamation by word and enactment by deed. These must complement and cross-fertilize each other."[55] Garrett, using the analogy of marriage to describe the intimate relationship of evangelism and social involvement, concludes, "As in marriage, so in this crucial issue, 'What therefore God has joined together, let no man put asunder' (Matt 19:6b, RSV)."[56]

EVALUATION OF GARRETT'S "MISSION" THEME

The second part begins the evaluation of Garrett's works on "mission" in order to demonstrate the close connection between his view of church mission and his notion of the priesthood of all believers. Stated otherwise, the mission of the church—universal evangelization, Christian unity, and social services—evinces a threefold character of the universal priesthood, namely, universalization, mediation, and obligation.

Universalization

In Garrett's ecclesiology, the mission of the church reflects the universal nature of the Christian priesthood. Church mission is universal because of the "purposive movement" of the eternally triune God who called, consecrated, and commanded a distinct and distinctive people, a kingdom of priests, for the purpose of saving and blessing other peoples.[57] Hobbs calls

54. Ibid., 56–57.
55. Ibid., 60–61.
56. Ibid., 62.
57. Garrett, "Authority for the Christian World Mission," 74–75; idem, "Biblical Doctrine of the Priesthood of the People of God," 139.

this calling the "missionary covenant" (Exod 19:5–6), a covenant that was renewed in Christ (1 Pet 2:1–10), and explained that "every believer is a priest charged with carrying out the [missionary] covenant."[58] Hobbs, however, roots the priesthood of the "believer" in the principle of "soul competency," the notion that "every person, or soul, is competent to stand before God without any need for a human or human-made 'go-between' . . . without the need of a human mediator or institution, ecclesiastical or political."[59] This interpretation is the foundation for the modern "direct access" conception—every Christian as his own priest approaches God's throne without human mediators or institutions except through Christ alone—a view which Garrett vehemently rejects as a candidate for the essential meaning of the "royal priesthood."[60]

As discerned from Garrett's works, all Christians as distinctive members of the "royal priesthood" are called by the Trinity to carry forth the universal mission. Unlike Hobbs, who bases the priesthood of the "believer" on soul competency, Garrett perceives that the "purpose" of the Father, the "propitiation" of the Son, and the "powerful presence" of the Holy Spirit constituted the universal priesthood (i.e., the church) and its universal evangelization.[61] The mission of the Christian priesthood is to proclaim the universal gospel of Christ (1 Pet 2:9) that will eventually result in a universal priesthood consisting of various peoples worthy for the worship and service of the triune God (Rev 4:11; 5:8–9; 20:6).[62] For Hobbs, soul competency is the foundation for Christian priesthood, but for Garrett the works of the Trinity are the fundamental elements of the priesthood doctrine of universal mission.

The distinct and unitive works of the triune God, rather than soul competency as the ground of the priesthood of believers, are means of combating individualism. Garrett decries the individualistic interpretation of the priesthood of "the believer," which often focuses on one's direct access to God, private interpretation of the Bible, or personal right to vote in church business meetings, and which often leads to a theological

---

58. Hobbs, *You are Chosen*, 80.

59. Ibid., 1, 3.

60. Garrett, "Priesthood of All Believers," 4. The doctrine of "direct access" primarily belongs to the high priesthood of Christ (Heb 4:14–16), not of Christians. See also footnote 38 in chapter 1.

61. Garrett, "Authority for the Christian World Mission," 74–76.

62. Ibid., 74–78.

and ecclesiastical Babel.⁶³ Yarnell convincingly argues that there was a distinct shift in the understanding of the priesthood doctrine from the early to the modern Baptists, of which the latter "redefined it with rugged individualism."⁶⁴ Logically, according to the doctrine of soul competency—the capacity to deal with God directly—the Christian priesthood is necessarily unnecessary because any kind of mediation is contradictory to individual soul competency.⁶⁵ The result of this individualistic reading is not the "priesthood of *all believers*" but "the priesthood of *the believer*,"⁶⁶ which elevates individual status and privilege. As perceived in Garrett's writings above, the priesthood of believers in the framework of the calling of the Father (Exod 19:5–6), the sending of the Son (John 20:21), and the empowering of the Spirit (Acts 1:8) emphasizes the service and accountability of all Christians—mutual ministry in the church and universal mission to the world.

A Trinitarian basis for the universal priesthood is evident in Garrett's earlier works on mission in the 1960s, but there seems to have been a significant shift in the later writing on mission in the 1990s. By comparing the earlier articles, "Authority for the Christian World Mission" (1963) and "Evangelism for Discipleship" (1964), with the later chapter on "Mission of the Church(es)" in his *Systematic Theology* (1995), the Trinitarian theme in mission is significantly omitted in the latter.⁶⁷ This does not mean that the specific works of the triune God play no role in the mission of the church. The mission of the Trinity as the foundation of Christian world mission is indisputable, but it seems to become an *implicit* foundation in Garrett's later explication of church mission. Nonetheless, the "universalist" elements as found in both the Old and New Testaments continue to permeate the chapter in his *Systematic Theology*. The universal purpose of God to include all nations in the worship of Yahweh began unfolding with the call of Abraham (Gen 12), of Israel (Exod 19:5–6; Isa 42:6–7; 49:6), and eventually of the church (1 Pet 2:9–10). Founded on the gospel of Christ, the church was promised the power of the Holy Spirit to take the gospel to both Jews and Gentiles (Acts 1:8), and ultimately to every

---

63. Garrett, "Recovering My Priesthood," 14.
64. Yarnell, "Changing Baptist Concepts of Royal Priesthood," 236.
65. Ibid., 246–47.
66. Ibid., 249.
67. Garrett, "Authority for the Christian World Mission," 74–76; idem, *Evangelism for Discipleship*, 37, 44, 68–69; idem, *Systematic Theology*, 2:527–44.

people group on earth.[68] This "universalist" emphasis is not a coincidence but a correspondence to Garrett's theme of the universal priesthood—that all God's people have been called to carry the universal gospel to all humanity through the world mission.

Mediation

Garrett's emphasis on the entire church as God's "mediatory witness" is also interconnected with the priesthood of all Christians. Historically, Garrett has pointed out that the emergence of missionary societies in the nineteenth century was, on the one hand, an abnormality of the church, and on the other hand, a judgment upon the church for not fulfilling its task as the agency of the gospel. Consequently, the universal mission of the entire church of God fell into the hands of a few members. In the twentieth century, however, Christian churches began to realize their role of gospel mediation.[69]

Jesus Christ the High Priest is indisputably the one and only mediator between God and people, but his people are the "mediation" of his gospel. Garrett states, "The Son's mission is the ground of his commissioning disciples . . . The Christian world mission is nothing less than God's witness by human instruments to his self-disclosure, directed to the least, the lost, and the last of mankind."[70] In addition, the Holy Spirit is the indispensable "Agent" of God to convict, convince, convert, consecrate, and consummate,[71] and yet the church empowered and indwelt by the Spirit is the "agency" of God's mission. Garrett rightly recognizes the vitality of the Holy Spirit sent by the Father and the Son in relation to the existence, unity, worship, and especially, mission of the church.[72] As Jesus is the "Mediator" and the Spirit is the "Agent," God's whole people are the "mediation" or "agency" of God's mission in Christ through the Spirit.

Christians, individually or collectively, are God's agents, instruments, or mediations of the universal gospel because they belong to God's chosen priesthood. Garrett's emphasis on mediation in connection to the priesthood theme is particularly evident in the following statements:

68. Garrett, *Systematic Theology*, 2:527–31, 537–41.
69. Ibid., 2:543–44.
70. Garrett, "Authority for the Christian World Mission," 76–77.
71. Garrett, *Evangelism for Discipleship*, 44–45, 68–69.
72. Garrett, *Systematic Theology*, 2:198–206.

> Who then are the proper agents or instruments for such universal witness? The biblical answer is clear. All Christians are to be agents of our Lord Christ's world mission. These upon whom the Holy Spirit has come are to be his witness (cf. Acts 1:8). All who belong to "a chosen race, a royal priesthood, a holy nation, God's own people" are, according to the divine intention, to "declare the wonderful deeds of him who called" them "out of darkness into his marvelous light" (1 Peter 2:9, RSV). The mission ought to have as its agents the whole people of God (1 Peter 2:10).[73]

On another occasion, Garrett gives a similar argumentation concerning the Great Commission in Matthew 28:19:

> The principal action of this commission is the making of disciples or "disciplizing." Those on whom the Holy Spirit has come in power are to be witnesses of Jesus (Acts 1:8). All who are privileged to be among "a chosen race, royal priesthood, a holy nation, God's own people" are responsible to "declare the wonderful deeds of him who called" them "but [sic] of darkness into his marvelous light" (1 Peter 2:9, RSV). Witness for the sake of making disciples belongs to the whole "people of God" ,λαὸς θεοῦ. (1 Peter 2:10).[74]

The two parallel statements above manifest two significant points: First, Garrett is emphatic that all believers are "missionaries," not just the clergy, pastors, or other church staff members. The "people of God" is created by and called for the mission of Christ. When each and every Christian realizes and acts upon the privilege and obligation as God's gospel agents, the potential outcome may be a new reformation of the modern Christian churches.[75] All Christians participating in the universal priesthood of evangelism are like, in Hobbs's illustration, a pipe organ with hundreds of pipes of various sizes, heights, and tones:

> When all of the Lord's people, great and small, sound in response to the Master's hand and in the power of the Wind of God, the result is a symphony of service that gladdens the heart of God. No matter what we may think of ourselves, each of us is important in God's purpose. So let your pipe play![76]

---

73. Garrett, "Authority for the Christian World Mission," 80.
74. Garrett, *Evangelism for Discipleship*, 59.
75. Garrett, "Authority for the Christian World Mission," 82.
76. Hobbs, *You are Chosen*, 82.

Second, Garrett appears to connect the role of the Holy Spirit with the function of all Christians in mission. A Pentecostal theologian rightly calls attention to "the lack of the role of the Spirit" in the Protestant concept of the Christian priesthood.[77] Such is not the case in Garrett's doctrine of the church and its mission. For instance, immediately after dealing with the meaning of *laos* in 1 Peter 2:10 as applied to all Christians, Garrett quickly points out what Paul envisioned in Ephesians 4:11–12 concerning the universal "gifts" of the Spirit—that church ministry was open to all Christians, yet some were gifted to equip all fellow Christians, who also received their various gifts, for the work of perfecting the body of Christ.[78] Then, Garrett immediately follows up this understanding with the concept that all "Christians as 'the people of God' ought to share in the Christian world mission," based on the mission of Christ.[79]

Garrett has been aware of the essential connection between the lordship of the Spirit and the common ministerial or missional role of all believers.[80] History shows that the institutional church frequently took captive the Holy Spirit and confined his role to clerical circles or certain theological foci, thereby ignoring the Spirit's work in the universal evangelization by the whole people of God.[81] Kärkkäinen also notices that in the history of Christian ministry the sovereign role of the Spirit has generally been restricted to the areas of "Word and sacraments," which happened to be designated as "the functions of the ordained clergy," rather than being open to all believers.[82] By remedying the problem of the "captive Spirit," Muthiah argues that the aspect of universal gifting or "charisms" is the key element to a holistic understanding of the biblical priesthood.[83] The universal priesthood, in the context of the Holy Spirit's diverse and universal "charisms," underlines both individual uniqueness and corporate identity. Every single Christian is gifted differently; therefore, all members of the church are responsible to exercise their "charisms" interdependently for the edification of the church as a whole,

---

77. Kärkkäinen, "Calling of the Whole People of God into Ministry," 145.

78. Garrett, "Authority for the Christian World Mission," 80.

79. Ibid., 80–81.

80. Garrett, *Systematic Theology*, 2:218.

81. Ibid., 2:207–9.

82. Kärkkäinen, "Calling of the Whole People," 153.

83. Muthiah, *Priesthood of All Believers*, 68. Muthiah's thesis is basically similar to the argument of his mentor. See Kärkkäinen, "Calling of the Whole People," 150–53.

the body of Christ, just as all the three persons are responsible for the life of the Trinity.[84] Unlike Muthiah, Garrett does not make the "charisms" to be the key element in the priesthood doctrine, nor does he embrace the idea that all believers who receive "charisms" are to be ordained.[85] Like Muthiah, Garrett affirms that all Christians are diversely empowered or endowed by the Holy Spirit; therefore, the entirety of the ordained and the laity are obliged to fulfill the ministry and mission of the church.[86]

Obligation

Garrett's view on Christian mission portrays not only the universal and mediatory character, but also the obligatory nature of the whole Christian priesthood. Garrett and Hobbs agree that the priesthood belongs not to an individual or certain Christians but to all Christians.[87] Garrett pointedly argues that the New Testament texts (1 Pet 2:4–10; Rev 1:5–6; 5:9–10) only use the plural form of "priesthood" or "priests" but never the singular "priest." Furthermore, the word "priest" is found neither in the lists of "spiritual gifts" nor of "leadership qualifications"; therefore, the New Testament priesthood is universal in essence.[88] Furthermore, Garrett is unambiguous on the matter that all Christians participating in the believers' priesthood are obliged to bring the gospel to the world. In his brief historical survey of the "Mission of the Church(es)," Garrett stresses that the Great Commission is obligatory to all Christians anytime and anywhere.[89] This means that both the believer who is an ordained pastor working full-time in the church and the lay Christian at her office, school, or home ought to carry out the Great Commission. All who belong to the "royal priesthood" are called to proclaim Christ: "The mission ought to have as its agents the whole 'people of God' (1 Pet 2:10)."[90]

---

84. Muthiah, *Priesthood of All Believers*, 68–71, 118.

85. Ibid., 85.

86. Although the Catholic Church has attempted to increase the participation and responsibility of the laity, there still exists a division of works between the laity and the clergy; the former is for the mission "in the world" and latter for the works "in the church." Both the "mission" to the world and the "ministry" in the church should be open to all Christians (Kärkkäinen, "Calling of the Whole People," 154).

87. Hobbs, *You are Chosen*, 12.

88. Garrett, "Biblical Doctrine of the Priesthood," 146–47.

89. Garrett, *Systematic Theology*, 2:542–43.

90. Garrett, "Authority for the Christian World Mission," 80.

Nevertheless, Garrett and Hobbs differ as to whether a Christian is primarily a priest to others or to oneself. Hobbs is critical of the idea that "every Christian is someone else's priest, and we are all priests to one another" because it omits what Hobbs accents; namely, it disregards that every Christian has free or direct access to God and denies the principle of soul competency.[91] Garrett, however, accentuates the universal priesthood that resonates with the initial and essential calling of God, i.e., to be a kingdom of priests for the sake of reaching others (Exod 19:5–6; 1 Pet 2:9–10). For Garrett, the Christian priesthood mission involves being priests to fellow Christians and to humanity in general. The former is reflected in his writings on Christian unity and the latter on social involvement.[92]

Garrett is correct to hold that church mission is closely related to church unity. Newbigin observes that church mission and unity are "indissolubly connected" because "the Church is that body in which God wills to reconcile all humankind to himself"; mission from an ecumenical perspective regards the church itself as "something sent into the world, the continuation of Christ's mission from the Father . . . the embassage of the whole people of God to the whole world."[93] Garrett argues in a similar vein that Christian unity is not a human concoction but divine will and mission.[94] All Christians—Jews and Gentiles—became the new people of God, the church of Christ. Garrett states elsewhere,

> The New Testament concept of the church includes much more than the determination of the local and non-local usages of ἐκκλησία. The church mentioned in Matthew 16:18 is emphatically Christ's assembly, not the assembly of national Israel. Yet Christians are "the Israel of God" (Gal 6:16).[95]

Despite distinct differences, Christians are consecrated and conjoined as God's new priesthood to fulfill the mission of reconciliation—not

---

91. Hobbs, *You are Chosen*, 14, 28. Hobbs does not deny that the Christian priesthood involves the responsibility for others—ministering to fellow Christians and reaching the non-Christians for Christ, but for him the primary meaning of the doctrine is "direct access" based on the principle of soul competency.

92. See the reviews above on "Ecumenism: Christian Unity" and "Ethics: Social Services."

93. Newbigin, *Trinitarian*, 11–12, 17.

94. Garrett, "Chapel: April 11, 1997."

95. Garrett, "Ecclesiology," 6.

only for universal evangelism, the divine-human reconciliation, but also for Christian unity, the human-human reconciliation.[96] Christian unity is not an option but an obligation of the whole Christian-priests to reach out to fellow Christians.

Christian-priests, individually or corporately, are also obliged to minister to non-Christians or people who are outside the church. According to Garrett, universal evangelism and "social services" are intimately related like a married couple.[97] As the church of God, there is not an option to choose either gospel proclamation or ethical conduct; both good news and good deeds are to be balanced and maintained as the mission of the whole people of God.[98] On the one hand, placing sole emphasis on evangelism to the neglect of social involvement may result in proclamation without significant effects on human society.[99] Newbigin urges the whole "lay membership of the churches," who have the closest and daily contact with cultural, political, social, economic, and educational life, to engage in "specific acts which challenge the existing structures and witness to the true purpose for which God created them."[100] Concurring with Newbigin, Garrett enjoins the churches, individually or collectively, to engage in helping, improving, or even changing human society.[101]

On the other hand, placing sole emphasis on serving humanity may result in the "social gospel" without accepting the ultimate sufficiency of Christ. Newbigin observes and warns against the possibility of denying the "uniqueness, sufficiency, and finality of Jesus Christ as the one Lord and Savior of the world" in the name of ecumenism, the movement that often changed Christian mission into mere social works to the "less fortunate, the unenlightened, the underprivileged" or to "the poor, the ignorant, the diseased."[102] Similarly, for Garrett, social services are not an alternative but a responsibility intimately attached to universal evangelism. Garrett's both/and approach to universal evangelization and social

---

96. Garrett, *Christian Doctrine of Reconciliation*, 1–4, 25–29.
97. Garrett, "Evangelism and Social Involvement," 62.
98. Ibid., 61.
99. Ibid., 59.
100. Newbigin, *Trinitarian Doctrine*, 61–62.
101. Garrett, "Evangelism and Social Involvement," 56–57.
102. Newbigin, *Trinitarian Doctrine*, 16–18.

services consistently revolves around the obligation of all Christian-priests to others for the reconciliation of the divine-human and of the human-human.

Furthermore, the mission of reconciliation of all believers aims at making disciples. Garrett calls it the "disciplizing responsibility of all Christians."[103] This "discipleship" emphasis is not an isolated theme addressed sporadically but a dear and deep concern of Garrett. In the early 1960s, this Southern Baptist theologian recognized the terrible dearth or absence of a careful study of the "discipleship" theme.[104] His work on "Evangelism for Discipleship" represents an early attempt to study carefully biblical discipleship.[105] Notwithstanding the gracious works of the Father, the Son, and the Holy Spirit as fundamentally indispensable in believers from generation to sanctification, Garrett is emphatic about the duty of the "disciplined discipleship" of all Christians, aimed at Christlikeness.[106] According to Garrett, Christlikeness embraces Christian unity.[107] Christian unity is the intention of the triune God and the mission of the people of God for the purpose of the reconciliation of both the God-human and of human-human relationships. No church should be limited to the one-sided work of evangelism, but should engage cooperatively in the efforts for Christian unity and exemplary ethics as essential features of the church's "universal" mission. In addition, Christian churches ought to employ "all available and legitimate means" (1 Cor 9:22), which may involve proactivity, creativity, and technology for the fulfillment of the world mission.[108]

While recognizing the spiritual commonality and responsibility of the entire Christian church to universal evangelization, Christian unity, and social services, Garrett is reluctant to abandon the Baptist distinctives, the *raison d'être* (e.g., believer's baptism, regenerate membership,

---

103. Garrett, *Evangelism for Discipleship*, 59.

104. Ibid., 51.

105. Thirty years later, Garrett revised *Evangelism for Discipleship* (1964) for his *Systematic Theology* (2:377–386), entitled "Discipleship" under the doctrine of the Christian life.

106. Garrett, *Evangelism for Discipleship*, 5. Despite clear distinction, discipleship is closely related to sanctification. Although the former is the responsibility of Christians and the latter the work of the triune God, both aim at "Christlikeness" (see 51–53, 72–73).

107. Ibid., 73.

108. Garrett, "Authority for the Christian World Mission," 78.

congregational polity), in the name of organizational unity or humanistic effort. By holding firmly to his Baptist convictions, Garrett is certainly not acting against the doctrine of the believers' priesthood, but rather he is obliged to be faithful to the doctrine, namely, to hold to what the Christian priesthood entails—believer's baptism, church discipline, congregational polity, and church-state separation. Adapting and alluding to Luther's words, Garrett states, "We love all those who in sincerity love and serve our common Lord, but God helping us, here we stand! We can do no other."[109] Like Luther who fought unwaveringly for the doctrine of justification by faith alone, Garrett attempts to follow faithfully the doctrine of the universal priesthood.[110]

CONCLUSION

This chapter notes three main concerns of Garrett's ecclesiology: first, the universal element—the mission of the church belongs to all churches and Christians, who are called and commanded by the triune God to bring the gospel to the whole world; second, the mediatory function—all Christians, clergy or laity alike, as God's people are agents of the gospel of Christ in the power of the Spirit to fulfill the mission of the church; third, the obligatory aspect—the mission of the church involves not only universal evangelism (i.e., divine-human reconciliation), but also church unity and social efforts (i.e., human-human reconciliation), all of which are the intention of God and the obligation of the churches. In conclusion, the three foci of Garrett's mission—"evangelization," "ecumenism," and "ethics"—consistently revolve around the threefold character of universality, obligation, and mediation of the universal priesthood. All Christians, as the distinctive instruments of the triune God, are obligated to fulfill the Great Commission of discipleship to all people, at all times, and by all means.

---

109. Garrett, "Ecclesiology," 8.
110. As an example, see Garrett, "Luther's Developing Doctrine of Baptism," 214.

chapter 3

The Membership of the Church

INTRODUCTION

THIS CHAPTER ATTEMPTS TO show that Garrett's writings on the theme of church membership consistently correspond to the nature and function of the believers' priesthood, particularly to the aspects of regeneration-baptism, confession-commitment, and discipline-discipleship. First, the present writer provides a review of Garrett's notion of church membership, which essentially involves the concepts of the "believers' church," "believer's baptism," and "born-again membership." The subsequent section will place Garrett's view of "membership" in an evaluative dialogue with three recent ecclesiologists—Peter J. Leithart,[1] Miroslav Volf,[2] and John S. Hammett,[3] so as to shed light on Garrett's membership theme in relation to his priesthood doctrine.

---

1. Leithart is a Presbyterian-Reformed theologian who is productive not only academically, but also domestically—he has ten children! For further information about Leithart's background and publications, see his faculty biography for New Saint Andrews College, "Peter J. Leithart, Ph.D." Online: http://www.nsa.edu/academics/peterleithart.php; or see his personal website, "About Peter J. Leithart, Ph.D." Online: http://www.leithart.com/about.

2. Volf, currently professor of systematic theology at Yale Divinity School, is a member of the Episcopal Church in the U.S.A. For further details on Volf, see his faculty biography page for Yale, "Miroslav Volf," Online: http://divinity.yale.edu/volf.

3. Hammett is currently professor of systematic theology at Southeastern Baptist Theological Seminary.

BELIEVERS' CHURCH CONCEPT

As then professor of theology at Southern Baptist Theological Seminary, Garrett played a significant role in initiating and organizing the first Conference on the Concept of the Believers' Church in June 1967. This "undelegated conference with voluntary participation" from various Christian denominations was to consult cooperatively or consider "together that which they hold in common and that on which they differ" by means of listening and responding to the "addresses of a historical, theological, and contemporary nature on the Church as the People of God."[4] Garrett distinctly introduces the concept of the "Believers' Church" in relation to the "indispensability of voluntary churchmanship with its many implications."[5] Although Garrett was responsible for editing *The Concept of the Believers' Church*,[6] his understanding of the Believers' Church or believers' churches can be better gleaned from his *Systematic Theology*.

Though the two terms are often used synonymously, "believers' churches" is distinct from the designation "free churches." The latter could refer to churches that are not established by any political government, or those which do not formally hold to any Christian creeds or confessions of faith, or those which do not keep the "historic liturgies or the ecclesiastical calendar."[7] The term "believers' churches" may imply any or most of the features above, but it particularly applies to the churches that are composed of "professing believers" only.[8] These professed ones are truly the "members" of the church of Christ. The term "member" is essentially not based on a social, political, or economic concept, but derived from the biblical analogy of one human body and its many "parts," as taught in 1 Corinthians 12:12.[9] Garrett explains that Paul used the "one body,

---

4. As stated in the abstract of Garrett, ed., *Concept of the Believers' Church*.

5. Ibid., 5. In the preface, Garrett distinguishes the capitalized "Believers' Church," conveying the ideal form of the church, from the "believers' church(es)," referring to the characteristics of the Believers' Church as expressed by any churches in history (7).

6. The book contains the addresses from the conference. Garrett, however, did not contribute a theologically substantial chapter to this book, except by providing a biographical sketch or a summary in each chapter; therefore, his view on the Believers' Church is not directly reflected here.

7. Garrett, *Systematic Theology*, 2:519.

8. Ibid.

9. "For even as the body is one and yet has many members, and all the members of the body, though they are many, are one body, so also is Christ" (1 Cor 12:12).

many members" analogy to explain the oneness of the body of Christ and the plurality of its believing members.[10] Such is the biblical rationale behind Garrett's view on *church membership*: "To be members of the body of Christ is to be members of the church of Jesus Christ."[11] Although the "body of Christ" and the "church of Jesus Christ" here, for Garrett, refer to the church in a "generic" sense, they, in this particular context, appear to have a "local" import: membership in the body of Christ is the theological ground for membership in a local church, and this local church membership belongs to true believers only who belong to Christ.

In his brief historical sketch of the believers' church heritage under the chapter "Membership of Churches," Garrett perceives the nature of the church as a disciplined community of professing Christians.[12] Every believers' congregation is responsible for receiving, discipling, nurturing, and even removing its members, including its ministers or pastors, if deemed necessary.[13] The latter, in particular, is a matter of church discipline or "disciplined churchmanship," an aspect which is integral to Garrett's ecclesiology, but has been neglected or even abandoned by many contemporary believers' churches.[14]

Garrett attempts not only to recover the practical dimension of discipline of church members, but also to lay a theological foundation for discipline as an essential aspect of the doctrine of the church and the biblical notion of discipleship—ecclesial discipline is intimately connected with the biblical concept of discipleship.[15] Though distinct in definition, the terms "discipline" and "discipleship" seem to be interchangeable in

---

10. Garrett explains succinctly, "The unity of the human body and the plurality of its members or parts are analogous, according to Paul, to the oneness of Christ's body and the plurality of its human members. To be members of the body of Christ is to be members of the church of Jesus Christ. Hence Christians, especially during the modern era, have often referred to *church membership*." (Garrett, *Systematic Theology*, 2:589); emphasis original.

11. Ibid.

12. Ibid., 2:599–602.

13. Ibid., 2:589, 590, 595, 596–600.

14. Garrett, *Baptist Church Discipline*, 1. It is beyond the scope of this chapter to discuss the details of church discipline presented in this book. The book will be closely examined in chapter 5, "Management of the Church." For the purpose of this present chapter, it is sufficient to point out that church discipline is an integral component to church discipleship and is the essential responsibility of the entire congregation.

15. Garrett, *Systematic Theology*, 2:597–98.

Garrett's explanations of the pertinent New Testament passages.[16] As a case in point, Garrett uses Matthew 18:15–17, which concerns specific ways of dealing with an offending member, to argue for church discipline as a significant aspect of discipleship.[17] "Discipling" church members involves positive and negative aspects of discipline. The positive aspect of discipline–discipleship, in a collective or corporate sense, has to do with the church members who "devoted themselves to the apostles' teaching and the fellowship, to the breaking of bread and the prayers (Acts 2:42, RSV)."[18] The negative aspect of discipline-discipleship ranges from admonition by individual Christians (Matt 18:15–17) to excommunication by the whole congregation (1 Cor 5). With regard to the latter, Garrett explains, "The principle is that the Christian fellowship is to 'judge' those inside the church and to 'drive out' (RSV, JB) the wicked person . . . from among them (1 Cor 5:9–13, esp. 11, KJV)."[19]

In summary, Garrett views a believers' church as a disciplined church of Christ made up of voluntarily professing Christian members who are responsible for the overall discipline-discipleship of the church. How does one become a member of a believers' church, and what does it mean to be such a member? The next two sections provide a review on the external symbol (i.e., believer's baptism) and the internal dimension (i.e., rebirth by the Holy Spirit) of church membership, as taught by Garrett.

BELIEVER'S BAPTISM BY IMMERSION

One's trusting in Christ as Lord and Savior and entering into the Christian fellowship as a "member" of Christ's body are visualized, symbolized, or actualized in believer's baptism by immersion.[20] In "The Theology and

16. Garrett points out a basic linguistic correlation: "the two English words 'disciple' and 'discipline' come from the same Latin verb, *discere*, 'to learn'" (ibid., 2:380).

17. Ibid., 2:597.

18. Ibid., 2:381. Garrett recognizes that discipline-discipleship has its individual or personal dimension: "Discipleship as *followship* [emphasis added] is intensely personal, for it means following the person, the will, and the example of Jesus" (379); a disciple is to be "under the continued instruction of Jesus as Teacher and Lord in the attitude of learning and applying the revealed will of the Master Teacher" in, for instance, "humble service" (John 13:5, 8), "brotherly love" (John 13:34–35), and "serious prayer" (John 11:1–4) (2:380). A disciplined disciple is to render full submission to Christ, which entails suffering and continuous abiding in Christ, resulting in "fruit-bearing" (2:380–82).

19. Ibid., 2:598.

20. For the purpose of this chapter, the present writer focuses only on water baptism

Practice of Baptism: A Southern Baptist View," Garrett surveys the history of Baptists with regard to baptism to argue that only professing believers should receive baptism by immersion, which is not only a physical sign of their obedience to Christ or of their testimony to faith in the gospel, but also a practice essential to the constituting of the churches.[21] In other words, true Christian congregations only consist of members who have been "immersed upon [public] confession of faith," which is called "close membership."[22] At the time of the writing, Garrett was particularly concerned with baptism administered to those who were under the age of nine, especially among those young children from Christian families.[23] Pertinent to the issue of receiving young children into church membership, Garrett raises the questions of, on the one hand, the solemnity or the validity of commitment made to Christ at a young age, and on the other hand, the possibility of moving toward infant baptism within the Southern Baptist churches.[24] Such a practice of baptizing young children may create further or later theological complication—the "rebaptisms" of those who had been baptized as young children.[25]

The prevailing pattern in the New Testament is that preaching, hearing, and the confessing of one's faith in the gospel of Christ precede water baptism (Mark 16:15–16; Acts 8:35–38; 16:30–34; 18:8).[26] Confession of faith is the condition for entering into the membership of the body of Christ. In Garrett's own words, "Interpreters of Paul agree widely that his

---

as depicted by Garrett. In general, Garrett holds to the view that Spirit baptism occurs at one's conversion, which is then followed by water baptism (see ibid., 2:180–85 for the aspect of baptism by/in/with the Holy Spirit).

21. Garrett, "Theology and Practice of Baptism," 65–68, 71. Garrett argues elsewhere, "In the Baptist confessions of faith extending from the seventeenth to the twentieth centuries one finds several statements of the meaning of baptism as ordinance: the sign of the believer's identification with the death, burial, and resurrection of Jesus; the outward sign of an inner cleansing or of the remission of sins; the sign of the eschatological resurrection of believers; *the sign of the believer's entry into the body of Christ*; a testimony both to believers and to nonbelievers; and an act of obedience to Jesus Christ" (idem, *Systematic Theology*, 2:578); emphasis added.

22. Garrett, "Theology and Practice of Baptism," 68.

23. Ibid., 71. Garrett does not disclose how to determine the "proper age" for Christian baptism, but one should note that Garrett himself was baptized when he was nine years old. See Garrett, "Baptist Identity and Christian Unity," 54.

24. Garrett, "Theology and Practice of Baptism," 71; idem, *Systematic Theology*, 2:577.

25. Garrett, "Theology and Practice of Baptism," 71.

26. Garrett, *Systematic Theology*, 2:575.

concept of baptism centers in union with Christ, involves *faith and entry into the community of faith*, calls for ethical transformation, and anticipates eschatological resurrection . . ."[27] Baptism is not a sacrament for it does not create faith; and yet, *conscious and confessed faith as symbolized in water baptism is externally essential to church membership, which inevitably entails commitment to discipleship.*[28] Garrett emphasizes that the Great Commission (Matt 28:18–20) is distinctly a command to "baptize those who have become disciples 'in the name of the Father and of the Son and of the Holy Spirit.'"[29] Stated concisely, commitment to discipleship is decisively connected with the call for baptism.[30]

In his recent article on baptism, Garrett once again raises the question of baptizing young children and admitting them into full church membership, especially those who are six years old and younger.[31] The heart of the matter is that, first, there is no distinctly biblical precedent for baptizing young children or infants; and second, there is the issue of the child's ability to make major life decisions at too young an age, such as marriage and career, much less the commitment to Christ.[32] For believers' churches, the rationale of the "age of accountability" plays a crucial part in baptism.[33] The concept of "accountability" is not just a matter of personal capability or responsibility in one's decision-making, but of conscious commitment to the corporate life of the church in discipline-discipleship, as entailed in church membership. Among other reasons, Garrett states pointedly that "infant baptism . . . has led to the primarily European phenomenon of the *Volkskirche* or *Staatskirche* (state church) with its great masses of *non-worshiping, non-practicing church members* who in effect have repudiated their baptism."[34] Precisely, paedobaptism or baptism, at very young age, of children without personal conviction

---

27. Ibid., 2:570; emphasis added.
28. See ibid., 2:570, 576; emphasis mine.
29. Ibid., 2:563.
30. Ibid., 2:564.
31. Garrett., "Baptists Concerning Baptism," 65. Garrett is certainly aware of the danger of setting an exact age for conversion or underestimating the capacity of responding to the gospel at any given age (Garrett, *Systematic Theology*, 1:584).
32. Garrett, "Baptists Concerning Baptism," 65.
33. For a detailed argument on the "age of accountability/discretion," see Garrett, *Systematic Theology*, 1:580–85.
34. Ibid., 2:577; emphasis added.

and commitment ultimately renders church membership inconsequential and ineffectual, especially with respect to discipline-discipleship and ministry-service.

Garrett also points out the issue of "alien immersion"—baptism by immersion administered by paedobaptist or non-Baptist churches.[35] Garrett seems to incline toward examining all applicants on a case-by-case basis; namely, "if personal faith and the biblical meaning of baptism have been validated," the receiving church should recognize the "non-Baptist immersion as true Christian baptism."[36] Negatively, Garrett regards as unbiblical the baptism of those who have had paedobaptism and later confirmation and of those who were baptized by a mode other than immersion.[37]

For Garrett, a believer's baptism by immersion upon one's confession and commitment of faith is the biblically, theologically, and historically external sign of entrance into full church membership. This external symbol, nonetheless, signifies the inner reality of the baptized Christian—regeneration by the Holy Spirit.

BORN-AGAIN MEMBERSHIP

In his earliest work on church membership, Garrett expressed his concern as well as conviction in this succinct title: "Seeking a Regenerate Church Membership," which, simply refers to the vital issue that "particular congregations of Baptists are supposed to be composed only of those who have given and do continue to give evidence of having been 'begotten' or 'born anew' or 'born from above' by the Holy Spirit."[38] While being adamant about believer's baptism by immersion as the visible symbol for church membership, Garrett is, in fact, seeking the essential evidence of

---

35. Garrett, "Baptists Concerning Baptism," 65–66. See Garrett, *Systematic Theology*, 2:581–82 and *Baptist Theology*, 213–48, for a brief historical sketch of the issue of "alien immersion" in Landmarkism. Landmarkists (e.g., James M. Graves, James M. Pendleton) refused to recognize baptisms or to accept preachers from non-Baptist or paedobaptist churches, based on the primary reason that, in light of the unbroken Baptist successionism, local Baptist churches were the only true churches which could administer valid baptism by immersion. See Brackney, "Landmarkism," 331–33; Noll, "Landmarkism," 669–70.

36. Garrett, "Baptists Concerning Baptism," 66.

37. Garrett, *Systematic Theology*, 2:582.

38. Garrett, "Seeking a Regenerate Church Membership," 25.

regeneration by the Holy Spirit, the integral foundation for constituting a believers' church.

Garrett explains that 1 John clearly teaches the notion and practice of "regenerate life"—those who have been born again of God are to love one another continuously and to refuse to commit sin (1 John 3:9; 4:7; 5:18). This "regenerate life" is "*sine qua non*" for one to be part of the Christian community.[39] "Regenerate" membership does not mean that one has to be completely sinless in order to be admitted or maintained as a member (1 John 1:8). Garrett perceives realistically the biblical tension between the "ideal" and the "actual" holiness of the church of Christ, between the "regeneracy" and "degeneracy" of church members, the tension that necessarily called for church discipline in the earliest New Testament churches.[40] A truly regenerate church involves positive and negative discipline: positively, discipline is geared toward the edification of the body of Christ—commonly termed "discipleship"; negatively, it is a church's specific act of removing or disfellowshipping an impenitent person from the Christian community (1 Cor 5:5).[41]

From a historical perspective, Garrett attempts to show that "regenerate" people constituted the genuine believers' churches and the efficient Christian ministry thereof.

> In the Baptist and free Church tradition "regenerate membership" has meant that visible, particular, local churches ought as nearly as possible to consist only of regenerate persons who continue to live in fellowship with Christ and with their Christian brethren as reborn men.[42]

These churches focused on two aspects of the church's life: the admission of members and the maintenance of membership. The demonstration of a regenerate life—the conversion experience and ethical conduct—was essential for a person's admission to the Christian community. Without evidence of a continuously regenerate life, the "member" could face brotherly reproof, temporary suspension from the Lord's Supper, or excommunication from the Christian fellowship.[43] Garrett indicates that

---

39. Ibid., 26.
40. Ibid., 27.
41. Ibid.
42. Ibid.
43. Ibid., 27, 29, 30.

a believers' church with a regenerate membership and church discipline produces more authentic and efficient ministry because the church is a "disciplined community of committed Christians."[44]

The main challenges that hinder the formation of a true regenerate membership include: a lack of clear verbal confession and testimony of one's conversion experience as the newly baptized is received, especially among younger children; a dearth of distinct and strict doctrinal and ethical standards for church membership, especially among churches that focus on numerical growth or on moral conformity with the general society; and a negligence of both positive (i.e., discipleship) and negative (e.g., reproof) aspects of church discipline, directly affecting the degree of participation of the church members.[45] If churches do not deal with these issues adequately, they can expect an increasing obscurity in the relationship between the church and the state (or the "world") and between the church's ethical practices and society's moral norms. Churches can also expect an "increase of the number and proportion of *inactive, indifferent, uncommitted, undedicated Christians*" in church membership.[46]

First and foremost, for Garrett, is the call for "a recovery of the biblical doctrine of the church as the people of God (*ηo λαoσ τηεoυ*)."[47] Garrett accentuates the *responsibility of the whole congregation* to examine the potential members with respect to their conversion experience, doctrinal understanding, and ethical conduct; and to carry out church discipline-discipleship to encourage or ensure the active participation of the church members.[48]

EVALUATION OF GARRETT'S "MEMBERSHIP" THEME

This section begins to assay Garrett's writings on "church membership" in relation to the doctrine of Christian priesthood, especially to its aspects of regeneration-baptism, confession-commitment, and discipline-discipleship. By means of interacting with Leithart, Volf, and Hammett, one will notice a certain fundamental commonality between Garrett's notion of believers' churches and the believers' priesthood.

44. Ibid., 31.
45. Ibid., 31–33.
46. Ibid., 34; emphasis added.
47. Ibid., 35.
48. Ibid., 35–36.

Regeneration-Baptism

Garrett maintains that baptism by immersion upon the confession of faith is vital to constituting the true believers' churches. Nowhere, however, does Garrett explicitly mention that believer's baptism is essential to the priesthood of believers.[49] Yarnell rightly observes that the Bible nowhere shows the immediate connection between baptism and the Christian priesthood;[50] therefore, baptism does not belong among the primary features of the priesthood doctrine. Although there is a lack of explicit connection, one cannot deny that the "entrance into the royal priesthood logically correlates with entrance into the church through baptism," adds Yarnell.[51] Toward the beginning of his writing career, Garrett also indicated a delicate relationship of the baptized members and their priesthood—"visible saints" (i.e., locally gathered congregations of baptized Christian members), a concept used by the seventeenth-century English Baptists, are "members of the body of Christ" (1 Cor 12:27) or "a chosen race, a royal priesthood, a holy nation, God's own people" (1 Pet 2:9).[52] For Garrett, baptism, though not considered as the primary feature in his priesthood doctrine, is essential for admission to the local believers' congregations, or the visible body of Christ, and hence, the Christian priesthood.

Taking the phrase "our bodies washed with pure water" (Heb 10:22) to mean baptism, Leithart contends that Christian baptism, replacing or fulfilling the Aaronic priestly consecration, produces the "New Covenant priesthood," despite his recognition that Scripture does not explicitly mention such replacement or fulfillment, nor does it unambiguously speak of baptism in connection with the Christian priesthood.[53] All those "sprinkled" by the blood of Jesus and "washed" by water baptism are not only bestowed with "privileges of access beyond those of Israel's High Priests" (Heb 10:22), but also endowed with "priestly ministry" (9:14)—Christian

---

49. Garrett notes, "Yet in no New Testament text is an explicit connection made between baptism and priesthood" (Garrett, *Systematic Theology*, 2:610; footnote 33). On the other hand, Garrett observes that, in Baptist history, the priesthood doctrine was distinctly "expressed in believers' baptism" (ibid., 2:614).

50. Yarnell, "Priesthood of Believers," 240.

51. Ibid.

52. Garrett, "Outside the Church No Salvation," 7; see also Garrett, *Systematic Theology*, 2:518–19.

53. Leithart, "Womb of the World: Baptism and the Priesthood," 50–51, 54.

service which goes beyond the Old Testament distinction of priests and laypeople.[54] Like Leithart, Garrett is aware of the lack of an explicit statement on the relation of baptism and the Christian priesthood, and yet baptism is a logically and theologically imperative step into Christian community and priestly ministry, which are open to all people of God without distinction.

Garrett and Leithart agree that baptism is an essential and external step of entry into the membership of the church.[55] In fact, there is no major discrepancy between Baptists and other Christian denominations in asserting that baptism initiates a person into Christian community.[56] Nevertheless, Garrett and Leithart differ on the issue of exactly who should be qualified to be admitted to the Christian community and communion. Leithart argues that baptized infants are to be called Christians and to be allowed to participate in the Lord's Supper for the primary reason that baptism is one of the efficacious means by which the Spirit "forms and molds" an infant, making him Christian or Christlike.[57] Infant baptism accentuates that God's prevenient grace precedes human response or choosing. Leithart states,

> Far from being a weakness, this is one of the strengths of infant baptism for Reformed theology, since it shows that God's approach to us precedes any response we make. The Divine Gardener loves us, waters us, cares for us, tends us before we can produce a thank offering in return. Infant baptism thus highlights the prevenience of grace.[58]

Leithart says rather bluntly and plainly that baptizing infants is tantamount to speaking to infants so that they may eventually understand and respond.[59] Parents *do* know that their infants cannot understand what they say, but they still speak to them, especially with gestures of hugs, pats, or kisses. Through speaking with symbols, the parents establish personal relationships with the children, and the latter gradually

---

54. Ibid., 55, 63–64.

55. See Leithart, *Baptized Body*, 32, 38, 41.

56. Cross and Livingstone, eds., "Baptism," 150–52; baptism is defined as the "Sacramental rite which admits a candidate to the Christian Church" (150); cf. Hammett, "Regenerate Church Membership," 27.

57. Leithart, *Baptized Body*, 114–16, 129.

58. Ibid., 121.

59. Ibid., 127.

learn to understand and respond. Correspondingly, through the "visible word" of water baptism, God speaks to infants so that they may eventually come to establish loving and trusting relationship with God.[60] All the baptized infants are, therefore, to be "counted and treated" as Christians by parents and other church members so as to reaffirm the status of the baptized, making their baptism "effective."[61] Leithart further explains, "The status of 'member of Christ' that was conferred in baptism thereby becomes internalized as the baptized person, treated as a believer, comes to see himself as others see him, and comes to accept the obligations that the rite has imposed on him."[62] In theological terms, Leithart holds to the so-called "baptismal regeneration" doctrine, though with a sociological slant. Baptism effects a "rebirth" or a "new creation," an "ontological transformation" that makes a person "a member of the Christian priesthood," which is a new identity with a new responsibility.[63] According to Leithart, "priestly baptism," though not a guarantee of eternal or eschatological salvation, is the way to live out salvation: "Living the life of salvation *is* ministering in God's house; as baptism authorizes and deputizes to such ministry, it grants a share in the life of salvation."[64]

Unlike Leithart, who promotes "open membership," admitting all, young or old, who have gone through baptism, Garrett intransigently teaches "closed membership,"[65] according to which one must be voluntarily baptized by immersion as well as relate one's experience of conversion in order to be admitted to the church of Christ. Garrett views baptism as the physical symbol of the believer's regeneration or the spiritual conversion.[66] In contrast to Leithart, Garrett is no proponent of the doctrine of "baptismal regeneration,"[67] which often teaches the efficacious power of

60. Ibid., 10–11.
61. Ibid., 128.
62. Ibid., 128–29.
63. Leithart, *Priesthood of the Plebs*, 168–70.
64. Ibid., 172–73; emphasis original.
65. In his most recent article, Garrett provides some historical and theological reasons for closed membership in Baptist churches. In general, believers' baptism by immersion is the central Baptist distinctive, past and present; and the center of representation and proclamation of the gospel—the death, burial, and resurrection of Christ. Garrett, "Analysis: Should Baptist Churches Adopt Open Membership? No," 10.
66. Garrett, *Systematic Theology*, 2:584; idem, "Theology and Practice of Baptism," 68.
67. See also Bromiley, "Baptismal Regeneration," 135.

water baptism for the bestowal of faith, the remission of original sin, and the regeneration of a person, resulting in participation in the priesthood of the baptized.[68] This view holds to the validity of baptizing very young children, even those who are incapable of giving any confession of faith or narrating their conversional experience.[69] The Southern Baptist theologian, however, is to seek church members that are regenerated by the Spirit as visualized in baptism by immersion—the regenerate-baptized membership. Precisely, Garrett refuses to admit nonbelieving or nonprofessing people (i.e., infants or children) into full church membership, and therefore, into the Christian priesthood.

Garrett's strict position on "closed membership" is, in fact, consistent with his concept of the "believers' churches," which consists only of voluntarily professing or confessing believers.[70] More concisely, his view on the "believers' churches" resonates with his notion of the Christian priesthood—like the believers' churches, the common priesthood belongs not to all people in general but to professing believers only, based on the biblical notion that all Christian members are priests and vice versa.[71] The theologically viable and valid conclusion is that when one becomes a member of a church by believer's baptism, he inevitably participates in the common priesthood of the baptized.

Garrett and Leithart are in sharp disagreement regarding the proper candidates for church membership, but they seem to concur with the theological conclusion that water baptism is closely associated with a new

---

68. From a Catholic vantage point, the baptized are regenerate and consecrated into the "priesthood of Christ," but their priestly role seems to be limited; for example, the faithful are "capable of offering . . . the Eucharist sacrifice," but "*mediately* (through a priest)" (Parente, "Baptism," 30); emphasis original.

69. Garrett, *Systematic Theology*, 2:305–6.

70. One may safely deduce that if Garrett holds to "closed membership" vis-à-vis believer's baptism by immersion, the logical consequence is that he must also hold to "closed communion vis-à-vis believer's baptism by immersion"—"proper baptism would be the proper qualification whereby non-members would be expected to partake of the elements in the Supper." Garrett expounds that the nature of the Lord's Supper is about the fellowship between Christ and his church and among fellow Christian members (1 Cor 10:16–17). Garrett concludes, "[B]aptism was not the only requisite to partaking of the Lord's Supper in the believers' church heritage . . . [T]he partaker must be truly regenerated, or converted, be living an exemplary Christian life, and having a meaningful church relationship" (Garrett, *Systematic Theology*, 672, 676, 677).

71. Garrett, "Biblical Doctrine of the Priesthood," 146; idem, "Priesthood of All Believers," 4.

role and task, the Christian priesthood that is without racial, economic, social, or political demarcation.[72] This is the true character of the believers' churches and the believers' priesthood—the members of the body of Christ are plural in background and capability, but they are united in one new status and service, the priestly community and responsibility. For Leithart, however, baptism is so open that the factor of personal faith is virtually inconsequential or irrelevant, especially among infants. Garrett, on the other hand, argues for the professing and voluntary faith preceding water baptism.

Elsewhere, Garrett points out the inconsistency of Luther's views on the Lord's Supper and baptism in relation to faith—personal faith is requisite for participating in the Lord's Supper, but conscious faith is not required for baptism.[73] The latter clearly contradicts the New Testament pattern of belief-precedes-baptism. By the same token, Leithart seems to demonstrate the same oxymoron by virtually dismissing the faith factor and still considering the baptized as Christian-priests. "[B]aptism makes priests regardless of the faith of the baptized or of the minister of baptism. Rightly done, baptism inducts, *ex opere operato*, into the priesthood of the Christian church," states Leithart.[74]

In summary, water baptism is requisite for church membership. Baptism, in and of itself, does not qualify a person for church membership; baptism is an external expression of the internal reality of one's personal faith in Christ and regeneration by the Holy Spirit. Moreover, Garrett's writings manifest a fundamental correspondence—the regenerate-baptized members are constitutive of the true believers' churches and the royal priesthood. It is reasonable to infer that, for Garrett, the means by which one is to enter into the fellowship of Christians—whether Christ's body or the believers' priesthood—is to be reborn by the Spirit through faith in Christ alone as symbolized in voluntary baptism by immersion.

Confession-Commitment

Garrett indicates that the call for baptism into church membership is the call for confession of faith in Christ and commitment to the commands of

---

72. Leithart, *Priesthood of the Plebs*, 158–59, 174.
73. Garrett, "Luther's Developing Doctrine of Baptism," 214.
74. Leithart, *Priesthood of the Plebs*, 159.

Christ.⁷⁵ Confession and commitment are imperative to and constitutive of the believers' churches. Based on Matthew 18:20, Volf argues that the presence of Christ in his Spirit is the indispensable foundation of a church: "*Where two or three gathered in Christ's name, not only is Christ present among them, but a Christian church is there as well*"; and, "Gathering in the name of Christ is the precondition for the presence of Christ in the Holy Spirit, which is itself constitutive for the church."⁷⁶ Volf explicates that gathering in the "name of Jesus Christ" means that the assembled people profess Jesus as their "Savior" and "Lord"—the confession of faith and commitment to Christ are the two conditions that make a congregation a church.⁷⁷ First, the confession of faith necessarily involves both the cognitive specification of Jesus (i.e., correct doctrine) and personal identification with Christ (i.e., belief in his person and work). Second, the profession of faith in Jesus entails commitment "of those assembled to allow their own lives to be determined by Jesus Christ."⁷⁸ Without confession of faith in Jesus as the Savior—correct doctrine and personal belief, there is no church; without commitment to Christ as the Lord, there is no church either.⁷⁹

In the same vein with Volf, Garrett is concerned with restoring the believers' churches by building them upon serious confession-commitment. Volf explains that the confession of faith is to be expressed by water baptism "before others."⁸⁰ Professing faith is not just a personal matter—believing within one's heart; it has a public character—professing or proclaiming Christ to others (Rom 10:9–10). Baptism is essentially an interpersonal communication, telling others of one's faith in Christ and, simultaneously, inviting them to believe in him.⁸¹ Garrett and Volf converge on the notion that the biblical and visible expression of faith is the believer's baptism, through which one demonstrates conscious and convinced faith in Christ.

---

75. Garrett, *Systematic Theology*, 2:563–64.
76. Volf, *After Our Likeness*, 136, 145; emphasis original.
77. Ibid., 146–47.
78. Ibid.
79. Ibid., 146, 148.
80. Ibid., 149, 153.
81. Ibid., 149.

The agreement between Volf and Garrett is particularly conspicuous on these three interrelated aspects: regeneration presupposes faith; faith precedes baptism; and baptism entails membership in the body of Christ and the priesthood of believers.[82] Volf states articulately, "A person does not simply freely join a church, but rather is *reborn* into it."[83] By baptism, every believer participates in the Christian priesthood, asserts Volf.[84] In other words, when a person is baptized into church membership, this is a visible and symbolic indication that he is "reborn" or "regenerate" into the priesthood of the baptized. The precondition of admission to church membership and Christian priesthood is basically one, i.e., regeneration-baptism. Similarly, for Garrett, whether to become a member of a church or to participate in the royal priesthood, the procedure is logically one and the same, namely, to be regenerate through faith as signified by water baptism, or simply in Garrett's term, "regenerate membership." Upon the confession of faith, especially in baptism, a Christian not only cognitively acknowledges the correct doctrinal content, but also volitionally identifies with the person the content points to, Jesus Christ, who is the Savior and Lord of all; and with the body of Christ, the fellow Christians who corporately subordinate and commit themselves to the lordship of Christ—to be obliged to praise him (i.e., worship) and proclaim his gospel (i.e., witness).[85] It is, therefore, biblically inconceivable to confess Christ by faith without being baptized into his body and the priesthood. To confess Christ is to commit to Christ and his body; to trust in Christ is to be entrusted to serve Christ and his church.

While Garrett and Volf are in harmony on the notion of baptism as the call for confession and commitment to the body of Christ, they seem reluctant to assert the theological conclusion that baptism serves as "ordination" into the Christian priesthood. Yarnell also remarks that Scripture does not teach baptism as "ordination" into the priesthood.[86] On the contrary, Leithart, especially based on Hebrews 10:19–22 and 1 Corinthians 6:11, argues that baptism, common to all Christians, as the "ordination" to the general priesthood fulfills and even replaces the Aaronic "ordination"

---

82. Ibid., 153, 180.
83. Ibid., 180; emphasis original.
84. Ibid., 246.
85. Ibid., 149.
86. Yarnell, "Priesthood of Believers," 240.

to the particular priesthood.[87] Although Volf concurs that, in virtue of "common baptism, all have become priests," he distinguishes the ministry of "ordained officer holders" from that of the laity on the basis of their "respective charismata."[88] Comparable to Volf, Garrett shows no disagreement that baptism, the physical indication of the spiritual regeneration through faith, admits Christians into church membership and its priestly ministry,[89] but nowhere does he distinctively see baptism as "ordination" into the priestly ministry of the church.[90]

Though his writing shows no indication of "baptism as ordination," Garrett *does* draw a parallel between the functions of the Christian priesthood and the Jewish priesthood, and yet not without distinction. "The basic function of Christians as priests is derived from the basic function of priesthood as indicated by the functions of the Jewish priesthood . . . Obviously, [the latter was] to offer sacrifices to God in behalf of men."[91] Derivatively, the Christian priests are to offer continuous sacrifices, the spiritual ones, including public profession (1 Pet 2:9), corporate praise (Heb 13:15), intercessory prayer (Heb 13:18–19), and benevolent deeds (Heb 13:16). Garrett highlights astutely, "The highest function of our common priesthood is . . . in our bearing the burdens of our broken, oppressed, and suffering *brethren*."[92] All Christians as priests are obligated and committed to serve perpetually for the encouragement and edification of fellow Christian-priests.

Garrett recognizes that biblical baptism inducts Christians into the priestly function, but this does not necessarily mean that he holds to the concept of "baptism as ordination." The topic of "ordination" is distinct from the theme of baptism in his writings. As a case in point, in "Ministry of Churches" (chapter 74), Garrett distinguishes and entitles two main sections: "General, or Lay Ministry: Priesthood of All Believers" and

---

87. Leithart, "Womb of the World," 50–51, 64; see also Leithart, *Priesthood of the Plebs*, 87–132.

88. Volf, *After Our Likeness*, 246.

89. In Garrett's *Systematic Theology*, the chapters' consecutive arrangement—"Baptism" (chapter 73), "Membership of Churches" (chapter 74), and "Ministry of Churches" (chapter 75)—indicates that baptism entitles one to church membership and ministry.

90. See Garrett, *Systematic Theology*, 2:607–18, on the doctrine of the royal priesthood in relation to church ministry.

91. Garrett, "Priesthood of All Believers," 4.

92. Ibid., 4; emphasis added.

"Special, or Ordained, Ministry."[93] This division is sufficient to show that, for Garrett, baptism is not equivalent to "ordination," though the former is the basis of the latter.[94] Garrett rightly observes at the outset that the Christian priesthood (1 Pet 2:9) is initially rooted not in the Aaronic priesthood, but rather in the covenant of the "peoplic" priesthood (Exod 19:4–6), God's original purpose to create a "kingdom of priests" or the "people of God."[95] Indisputably, God's initiative in providing revelation and his loving election are the foundations of this priesthood, and yet it is preconditioned by the obedience and faithfulness of the people.[96] Here, Garrett indicates that "ordination" is not the primary precondition to the peoplic priesthood, but faith and obedience, which precisely underlie the meaningful symbol of baptism. Stated simply, baptism, as a symbol of confessed and committed faith, initiates believers into the community and priesthood of God. Thus, the justified inference is that, for Garrett, baptism does not essentially mean "ordination" into priesthood. Rather, baptism is the external mark of one's faith *confession* and faithful *commitment* to the commandment and the community of God.[97]

Paedobaptism is, therefore, ecclesiologically untenable because it denies one's voluntary confession of faith and creates noncommitted membership. Baptism of infants or young children breeds a *corpus permixtum* of mixed believing and nonbelieving membership,[98] a condition that not only distorts the true character of a believers' church, but also often contributes to the "inactive, indifferent, uncommitted, undedicated" membership.[99] On the other hand, admitting *confessed* believers by immersion into church membership directly and positively fosters the *committed* participation of not the select few, but the whole believing church.

---

93. Garrett, *Systematic Theology*, 2:604, 618.

94. See also Volf, *After Our Likeness*, 246. It is beyond the scope of this chapter to deal with the nature of ordination (or ordained ministry) in relation to the priesthood of all believers. The issue will be discussed in detail in chapter 4, "The Ministry of the Church," of this monograph. Presently, it is sufficient here to point out that baptism is not interchangeable or synonymous with "ordination" in Garrett's priesthood doctrine.

95. Garrett, *Systematic Theology*, 2:604.

96. Ibid., 2:604–5.

97. Ibid., 2:578–79.

98. Hammett, "Regenerate Church Membership," 24.

99. Garrett, "Seeking a Regenerate Church Membership," 34.

Discipline-Discipleship

As baptism is for believers only and initiates them into church membership, the call for baptism, in effect, entails commitment to communal discipline-discipleship, the essential function of the entire believers' church. Garrett would not disagree with the statement that, in the New Testament era,

> To be baptized and not to be a part of a local church was simply unthinkable... Baptists believe that a return to the New Testament practice of baptism of believers by immersion is essential for a true understanding of the nature of faith, and *discipleship*. The responsibilities of the church member include sharing in public worship, prayer, and church meetings and engaging in the evangelistic, educational, and caring life of the local church.[100]

The believers' church and its mission, like the Christian priesthood, properly belong not to the public or pastors only, but specifically to all regenerated-baptized Christians. Admitting, therefore, the nonconfessing children or the nonregenerate adults jeopardizes the true character of the believers' church and, consequently, its function as the people of God. Positively, Garrett recognizes that believer's regeneration-baptism is crucial to the committed and consistent participation in the priestly function of the church—offering "spiritual sacrifices" by participating in ministries of global evangelization, mutual service, and congregational discipleship.[101]

First, the mixed membership negatively affects the vital church mandate of evangelization, the primary priestly function to others.[102] On the one hand, the church that receives members without genuinely repentant faith or regenerate conduct often invites criticism from the world that the church is "full of hypocrites and members whose lives are no different from those of nonbelievers."[103] On the other hand, the "nonregenerate" members of the church are neither motivated nor obliged to evangelize

---

100. Garrett, ed., *We Baptists*, 28; emphasis added. *We Baptists* is a cooperative effort of the six Baptist World Alliance (BWA) study commissions. The statement above is not written by Garrett himself, but it, nonetheless, adequately portrays his view on the relationship between the significance of believer's baptism and the responsible discipleship of church membership.

101. Garrett, "Biblical Doctrine of the Priesthood," 148–49.

102. See chapter 2, "The Mission of the Church."

103. Hammett, "Regenerate Church Membership," 31.

because they themselves have neither believed in nor lived out the gospel. How could those who have not even believed persuade others to believe (cf. Rom 10:14–15)? Consequently, the church in its entirety will not be able to fulfill effectively the primary priestly function of the Great Commission because the church has innumerable, in Garrett's words, "non-practicing members who in effect have repudiated their baptism."[104]

Second, the mixed church is not only unable to evangelize effectively, but also cannot fulfill the call to mutual service. In a corporate sense, Garrett remarks that Christian members are to function as priests to others—evangelizing nonbelievers, and priests to each other—serving members mutually, rather than priests to themselves.[105] In the same token, Hammett points out that the genuine believers' church is able and ought to carry out the *diakonal* service of the Christian members—to serve others and one another, such as "to pray for one another, to teach and admonish one another, to counsel [and consult] one another, to edify and encourage one another, to love and forgive one another, and to serve and bear one another's burdens."[106] The nonregenerate members may try to do all the above, but not without pretense. Garrett depicts the care of members for one another in this manner, "Paul taught that even as in the human body to avoid 'schism,' 'the members' (KJV) 'have the same concern for one another . . . (1 Cor 12:25, TEV), so should it be in the body of Christ."[107] The "entire community of believers has the privilege and responsibility of mutual care"; every Christian is to be involved in the pastoral ministry of the church.[108] Garrett points out that the ultimate goal of mutual and communal service as a church is to conform to and form the image of Christ (Gal 4:19; Rom 8:29),[109] which is nothing less than the primary calling of the church to discipleship. The believers' church is a community of disciples to make disciples, simply because all of the chosen and royal priesthood of God are mandated to produce disciples.[110] Nevertheless, the nonconfessing or nonregenerate members are not in proper position to

---

104. Garrett, *Systematic Theology*, 2:577.
105. Ibid., 2:617.
106. Hammett, "Regenerate Church Membership," 23.
107. Garrett, *Systematic Theology*, 2:595.
108. Ibid.
109. Ibid.
110. Ibid., 2:383.

edify each other or disciple others. Hammett argues, "Ephesians 4:16 and Colossians 2:19 indicate that the body grows only when each part does its work, but if parts of the body are not regenerate, they will tear down the body rather than build it up."[111]

Third, the congregation that is mixed with nonregenerate membership creates issues of discipline. For those who are baptized at a very young age or who are immersed without confession of faith will likely show lack of regenerate conduct and participatory membership later in church life. This is not to imply that the believing-confessing believers are immune from spiritual backsliding or occasional sin after being baptized. Garrett recognizes the "regeneracy" and the "degeneracy" as the real tension of the regenerate members; therefore, it necessitates that the church implement positive and negative discipleship.[112] Specifically, the whole church carries the weight of responsibility to *examine* new members, to *edify* current members, or if needed, to *excommunicate* unrepentant members. Nonetheless, the church is unable to train those "nonconfessed-nonregenerate" members to be witnesses of the gospel as they themselves have not decidedly accepted it; nor urge them to pray for others sincerely as they have not confessedly trusted in the name of Jesus; nor admonish them to love one another sacrificially as they have not personally experienced the unconditional love of Christ; nor expect them to worship truthfully and fellowship meaningfully with others as they have not been regenerated by the Spirit of God. Strictly speaking, they become, in Garrett's expression, "non-worshiping, non-practicing" members.[113] The church will surely fall short of implementing consistent and effective discipline-discipleship until it chooses to restore regenerate church membership only.[114]

According to Garrett, since a believers' church is a disciplined community of professed Christians, all regenerate members are accountable for the common tasks, from receiving to restoring members, from discipling to disciplining members.[115] These responsibilities are expected

---

111. Hammett, "Regenerate Church Membership," 33.

112. Garrett, "Seeking a Regenerate Church Membership," 27.

113. Garrett, *Systematic Theology*, 2:577.

114. Hammett, *Biblical Foundations for Baptist Churches*, 105–7. Hammett states that regenerate church membership "is a prerequisite for effective church discipline and is protected by church discipline" (107).

115. Garrett, *Systematic Theology*, 2:589–601.

of the whole believing church, not just the elite or elect few. The notion of common and communal responsibilities basically resonates with the essence of the Christian priesthood that every baptized member has a mission or a ministry.[116] Since a believers' church consists of regenerate-baptized or confessed-committed Christians only, they are able to carry out responsibly the priestly functions. Hammett argues pointedly that the believers' church is able to manage or govern its church life because it is composed only of those who are regenerated, indwelt, and gifted by the Spirit in Christ.[117] "Since all believers are priests, and only believers should be members of the church . . . all these believer-priest church members are able to and responsible to help the church find God's direction for its life," states Hammett.[118] Garrett and Hammett concur that, by baptizing infants into church membership, the church creates not merely the issue of mixed membership of "regenerate and nonregenerate persons," but also ultimately the difficulty of fulfilling consistently and effectively the priestly functions of the church—evangelization, service, and discipline.[119]

In summary, nonconfessing and nonregenerate people demonstrate lack of spiritual adequacy and voluntary commitment to be church members. Only the regenerate members could fulfill responsibly and continuously the primary tasks of the church, which are none other than the functions of the Christian priesthood—gospel witness, mutual service, and discipline-discipleship.[120]

CONCLUSION

This chapter perceives three parallel relationships between Garrett's views of church membership and the doctrine of the Christian priesthood:

---

116. Ibid., 2:617.
117. Hammett, "Regenerate Church Membership," 28–29.
118. Hammett, *Biblical Foundations for Baptist Churches*, 46.
119. Hammett, "Regenerate Church Membership," 29–31.
120. This, however, is not to suggest that the church is to remove the nonconfessing members from the church building, but only from church membership. These people should become the object of love and care by the church members. The ultimate goal is to welcome them into the church of Christ on "Christ's terms, which include commitment to Christ and to his people" (Hammett, "Regenerate Church," 37). Hammett suggests some practical ways to recover the regenerate church membership through church covenant, believer's baptism, and redemptive discipline (idem, *Biblical Foundations*, 114–26).

First, Garrett's view of the nature of the believers' church corresponds to that of the royal priesthood. Both the church and the priesthood belong to neither a few pastors nor the general public, but to all regenerate believers of confessed and committed faith. The primary symbol of the voluntary confession and commitment of faith is believer's baptism by immersion. To believe in Christ without being baptized into his body of believers or without participating in the priesthood of the believers is unsustainable in Garrett's view of ecclesiology. Despite a definite distinction between the church and the priesthood in scope and definition, Garrett seems to see both the priesthood of believers and the believers' churches as belonging to the same group of localized and visible body of believers.

Second, Garrett's notion of the admission to the believers' church by baptism correlates with the entry into the priesthood of the believers by faith. By definition, there is a clear distinction between baptism by immersion and regeneration by faith, and yet they are theologically connected—baptism is a symbolic representation and a public confession of one's spiritual regeneration and voluntary commitment to Christ. Thus, only by belief-baptism is a believer admitted to the body of Christ. Similarly, one enters into the Christian priesthood by faith, and this voluntary faith is not without public confession and commitment to Christ and his church. The theological correspondence between the priesthood and the church is that one enters into both by means of the same twofold requirement: regeneration–baptism.

Finally, on the basis that all believers are priests and only believers are church members, the primary functions of the believers' church essentially concur with those of the Christian priesthood, which include world evangelism, mutual care, and disciplined discipleship. As the members participate in the task of the church, they are, in effect, fulfilling the priestly function of "spiritual sacrifices"—worship, prayer, witness, service, discipleship, and discipline by the whole congregation, not just by the pastors or the leaders. Being regenerated and indwelt by the Holy Spirit, they, as a fellowship of Christians, are privileged and responsible to help to direct the life of the Christian community, a task that distinctively belongs to all church members.

chapter 4

The Ministry of the Church

INTRODUCTION

THIS CHAPTER FOCUSES ON the theme of church ministry for the purpose of demonstrating that the ministry aspect, as understood by Garrett, is directly rooted in the character and essence of the Christian priesthood, particularly in the concepts of communality-mutuality, universality-diversity, and equality-complementarity. This writer will, first, provide an interpretative review of Garrett's three major dimensions of ministry—"The Priesthood of Christ," "The Priesthood of Christians," and "The Priesthood of the Specially Called." In the second main section, the attention will be on evaluating Garrett's view of ministry through interactions with one Roman Catholic theologian, Hans Küng, and three Baptist authors, namely, Walter B. Shurden, Stanley J. Grenz, and David S. Dockery.

THE PRIESTHOOD OF CHRIST

Garrett sets out to assert that the ministry of the church is founded upon, though not identical with, the ministry of Jesus Christ, the latter as traditionally expressed in the concept of *triplex munus*—the king-servant, the prophet-apostle, and the high priest.[1] With hindsight that the "priesthood of the people of Israel" in Exodus 19:4–6 is the basis of the "royal priesthood" of all Christians in 1 Peter 2:9, Garrett contends that

---

1. Garrett, *Systematic Theology*, 2:603, 611.

the "priesthood" motif in the book of Isaiah provides a transition to the New Testament doctrines of the priesthood of Christ and of Christians.[2] Succinctly, the threefold pattern of the Servant's royal (Isa 49:7; 52:12–15), prophetic (49:2; 50:4–5), and "priestly or sacrificial" (53:3–12) functions provide the basic framework for the ministry of the church.[3]

What precisely is the essence of Christ's threefold pattern for the ministry of his church? The answer seems to lie in the concept of servanthood or *diakonia*.[4] Garrett frequently demonstrates that the church's ministry is servant ministry. He quotes Torrance word-for-word, "It is indeed in terms of the suffering servant-ministry that we are to see the basic unity in the church's prophetic, priestly, and kingly functions."[5] Despite the fact that Jesus himself did not assume explicitly the title of priest or the idea of priesthood, Garrett observes the "priestly implications in Jesus' affirmed and enacted servanthood in the Gospels"—specifically, Jesus' ministry as the "Servant of the Lord" (Matt 12:17–21; Isa 42:1–4); Jesus' "self-giving service" as his central mission (Mark 10:45; Luke 22:27); Jesus' cleansing of the temple, "a house of prayer for all nations" (Mark 11:15–17), as "indicative of the universal nature of priesthood"; Jesus' referring to his disciples' "servanthood and followship" (John 12:20–26); Jesus' washing of his disciples' feet (John 13:1–17) as instituting them "into a royal priesthood"; and Jesus' Passover meal (Mark 14:17–26) as indication of his self-sacrifice and "priesthood."[6]

One cannot fail to see the high priesthood of Jesus in John 17 and the book of Hebrews,[7] but Garrett rightly warns that the priesthood of Christ is not identical with the priesthood of Christians.[8] By quoting Eastwood verbatim, Garrett once again accentuates the theme of servanthood, "While His priesthood is incommunicable, it is nevertheless the

---

2. Ibid., 2:604–7. See chapter 1 also for a summary of Garrett's explanation of the "priesthood" motif in Isaiah.

3. Ibid., 2:603, 607; see "Jesus as the Servant of the Lord (or, of God)," 1:646–51.

4. Garrett, "Biblical Doctrine of the Priesthood," 142–43, 146; idem, *Systematic Theology*, 2:603.

5. Garrett, *Systematic Theology*, 2:607; Torrance, *Royal Priesthood*, 87.

6. Garrett, *Systematic Theology*, 2:607–8. Here, Garrett mostly relies on Eastwood, *Royal Priesthood of the Faithful*, 38–43, for the priestly implications of Jesus in the gospels.

7. See Garrett, *Systematic Theology*, 1:657–59, for Garrett's explanation of "Jesus as High Priest," particularly on the book of Hebrews and John 17.

8. Ibid., 2:608.

pattern of that general servanthood and universal priesthood of those who by faith and obedience have chosen to become lowly servants of the divine will."[9] In a word, the priesthood of Jesus is characterized by self-sacrificial service for the sake of others—the prophetic, priestly, and princely servanthood, the pattern of ministry that Christ established for the Christian churches.

THE PRIESTHOOD OF CHRISTIANS

After pointing out the distinct *status* of Christians as priests (1 Pet 2:4–10; Rev 1:5–6; 5:9–10), Garrett turns the readers' attention to the *service* or the "sacrificial functions" of the Christian-priests—the "spiritual sacrifices" (1 Pet 2:5) as distinguished from ritual or temple sacrifices.[10] "Spiritual sacrifices" include witness, worship, stewardship, and service.

One of the primary functions of the priesthood of believers is witness, which involves personal testimony (1 Pet 2:9), missionary career (Rom 15:15–16), or sacrificial death—martyrdom—for the sake of the gospel (Phil 2:17).[11] Without doubting that global evangelization is the primary function of the universal priesthood, Garrett, nonetheless, accentuates the critical relationship between verbal evangelism and the Christian ministry of *diakonia*: "The modern era, at least from Carey's era, has sought to heal the bodies, instruct the minds, counsel the spirits, and strengthen the families of human beings through actions that transcend a strictly verbal proclamation."[12] In short, Christian witness involves a twofold function: speaking and service (1 Pet 4:11).[13]

Worship is another essential part of the priestly ministry of the church.[14] In his writings on the priesthood concept, Garrett repeatedly points out that worship, whether in the form of praising God (Heb 13:15), dedicating oneself (Rom 12:1), serving God (Heb 9:14), or praying for

---

9. Ibid., 2:609; Eastwood, *Royal*, 45–46.
10. Garrett, *Systematic Theology*, 2:609.
11. Garrett, "Biblical Doctrine of the Priesthood," 148–49.
12. Garrett, *Systematic Theology*, 2:545.
13. This writer has discussed in chapter 2, "The Mission of the Church," the task of mission in the form of evangelization (i.e., God-human reconciliation) and service (i.e., human-human reconciliation) as essential to the function of the believers' priesthood.
14. By definition, worship is recognition of God's preeminent worth (Garrett, *Systematic Theology*, 2:645) or the "service of praise, adoration, thanksgiving, and petition directed toward God through actions and attitudes" (McKim, "Worship," 307).

others (Heb 13:18–19), is the primary function of the fellowship of believers.[15] From his biblical exposition, Garrett discerns worship as "congregational." In the New Testament, Christian worship was unlike Jewish temple worship; the former had no use for the temple's "holy places" or "priests." Moreover, Christians transformed the Old Testament ritual sacrifices into "spiritual sacrifices" offered by all believer-priests (Heb 13:15–19).[16] Writing on the general characteristics of the early churches, Garrett asserts that "primitive Christian worship had no holy places but was congregational . . . Christians often worshiped together in private homes. Primitive Christian worship . . . knew no marked division between worship and 'work' or service."[17] One of the primary purposes of worship, according to Garrett, is "to equip worshipers for their mission and service in the world."[18] Garrett notes elsewhere that the term λατρεύειν ("to serve" or "to worship") in the New Testament was deliberately used in distinction to the "more levitically oriented term λειτουργεῖν."[19] Thus, worship is a ministry of servanthood opened to the entire Christian priesthood.

Stewardship is a third distinct aspect of the Christian priestly sacrifice.[20] In 1972, Garrett expounded a biblical rationale for Christian stewardship of material things. On the basis of "God's ownership of all things" as well as the human role of "dominion over lower creatures," Garrett emphasized "man's obligation to a responsible *management* or *use*

---

15. Garrett, "Biblical Doctrine of the Priesthood," 148; idem, "Priesthood of All Believers," 4; idem, "Recovering My Priesthood," 14. See also Garrett's writings on prayer: idem, "Prayer,"1102–3; idem, "Theology of Prayer," 3–17; idem, *Systematic Theology*, 2:429–47 (chapter 68). Among other things, Garrett stresses that prayer, essentially through Christ's high priestly intercession, is at once the "privilege and duty of all Christians"; to believe is to pray and to live is to pray (Garrett, "Prayer," 1102–3; "Theology of Prayer," 17).

16. Garrett, *Systematic Theology*, 2:647–50.

17. Ibid., 2:650.

18. Garrett concludes, "Worship needs to glorify the triune God, to awaken worshipers to the presence and leadership of God, to enliven and apply the biblical story, *to equip worshipers for their mission and service in the world*, and to quicken the anticipation of the last things" (ibid., 2:657); emphasis added.

19. Garrett, "Biblical Doctrine of the Priesthood," 148, footnote 34. For example, by the blood of Christ, Christians were sanctified for to. λατρεύειν θεῷ ζῶντι (Heb 9:14).

20. Garrett explains stewardship: "Gifts given by the Philippian Christians through Epaphroditus for Paul in his proclamation of the Gospel to the Gentiles are 'a fragrant offering, a sacrifice acceptable and pleasing to God' (4:18)" (Garrett, "Biblical Doctrine of the Priesthood," 149).

of material things—a concept translated from the Greek New Testament οἰκονομία by the English term 'Stewardship.'"²¹ Garrett incisively states:

> Material things, when freely and gratefully dedicated and given to God and entrusted to the Christian "household of faith," can and should be so utilized by Christian persons in the service of Christ and the fellowship of his church as to be means and instruments employed and empowered by the Holy Spirit for Christian evangelization, Christian instruction and nurture, and Christian helping ministries. Such gifts sustain both the enablers who seek to equip all Christians for their ministries and the emissaries of the good news of Christ who plant the need for new fellowships of the reborn.²²

While faithful stewardship applies to one's physical possessions, spiritual gifts, and ecological responsibilities, Garrett, in his *Systematic Theology*, specifically urges Christians to fulfill the obligation of the tithe with a willingness to serve and to support the works of their respective churches.²³ Giving the tithe to the church where they are formally members is a way of participating in the congregational ministry or common mission.²⁴ Garrett observes: "Strong *congregational life* and serious *congregational participation* in the world mission" rely on the tithing and the giving of the church members.²⁵ Christian tithing-giving is an act of worship, a characteristic of discipleship, and more significantly, an instance of congregational participation in the church's "educational and diakonal ministries" and "evangelistic and missionary outreach."²⁶

Fourth, Garrett propounds that "spiritual sacrifices" include "acts of benevolent sharing" or "ministering service."²⁷ As Hebrews 13:16 stated, "And do not neglect doing good and sharing, for with such sacrifices God is pleased." Garrett notes that the term "sharing" is translated from *koinonia* (lit. "fellowship").²⁸ Pertinent to the abovementioned *diakonia, latreia,*

21. Garrett, "Christian View of Material Things," 85; emphasis original.
22. Ibid., 94.
23. Garrett, *Systematic Theology*, 2:405, 419–22, 424–26.
24. Ibid., 2:424–25.
25. Ibid., 2:426; emphasis added.
26. Ibid., 2:427.
27. Garrett, "Biblical Doctrine of the Priesthood," 149; idem, "Priesthood of All Believers," 4; idem, *Systematic Theology*, 2:610.
28. Garrett, "Biblical Doctrine of the Priesthood," 149, footnote 36.

and *oikonomia*, the term *koinonia* also means nothing less than Christian servant-ministry to each other. This concept of ministering service is particularly akin to Garrett's teaching on the spiritual gifts—the various charisms, sovereignly given by the Holy Spirit, that ought to be properly used for the common caring for one another (1 Cor 12:7), for equipping fellow Christians for ministry, and/or for building up the "body of Christ" (Eph 4:12).[29]

Garrett rejects the priesthood view that either stresses "direct, unhindered access to God as the central meaning of the universal priesthood" or combines the "direct access" view with "servant ministry (or spiritual sacrifices)" to promote individualistic privileges or status (e.g., direct access to God in prayer, private interpretation of the Bible, or individual rights in a local church) as well as responsibilities.[30] Rather, he distinctly argues for "the offering of spiritual sacrifices as the essential function of the priesthood of all Christians" and concludes that "the privilege of direct access is a corollary of the high priesthood of Jesus."[31] Garrett emphasizes that believers' "highest priestly function is not basking in our privilege of access to divine mercy. The access to God's mercy and assisting grace follows from our Lord's high priestly office . . ." (Heb 4:14–16).[32] The priesthood of Christians essentially pertains to service rather than status.

THE PRIESTHOOD OF THE SPECIALLY CALLED

By underscoring the significance of the "spiritual functions" of the Christian priesthood as a potentially powerful means for church revival and renewal, Garrett does not by any means vitiate the church's ministry of the specially ordained. He approaches the ordained ministry by briefly pointing out the "differing functions of Old Testament leaders" and "the occasions on which hands were laid upon such leaders."[33] On the one hand, the royal, prophetic, and priestly functions were carried out separately by different Old Testament individuals, but these functions were

---

29. Garrett, *Systematic Theology*, 2:218. For details on Garrett's work on the spiritual gifts, see "The Holy Spirit and Spiritual Gifts" (chapter 56), 2:215–38.

30. Ibid., 2:616–17.

31. Ibid., 2:617.

32. Garrett, "Recovering My Priesthood," 14.

33. Garrett, *Systematic Theology*, 2:618.

once united in Abraham, Moses, Samuel, and more significantly in Jesus, whose threefold ministry became the pattern for the church's ministry.[34] On the other hand, the Old Testament priests (Exod 28–29; Lev 8–9; Num 8:10), prophets (Ps 105:15; 1 Kgs 19:16), kings (1 Sam 16:1–13), and other leaders (e.g., the seventy elders—Num 11:16–25; and Joshua—Deut 31:14–23) received consecration and/or ordination in the form of anointing with oil and/or laying on of hands.[35]

In the New Testament, Jesus specially appointed the twelve disciples as apostles for a "mission of teaching, preaching, and healing" (Matt 9:35—11:1), as witnesses to Jesus' resurrection (Acts 1:22), and for "the ministry of the word" (Acts 6:4). Garrett seems to contend for the cessation of this original apostolic office: "Any claims to the perpetuity of the apostolic office belong to the patristic era or later age."[36] Except for the apostolic office, Garrett, nonetheless, disagrees with the modern supposition that "[extraordinary or miraculous] gifts ceased to be given at the end of the apostolic age whereas others continue to be given."[37] Garrett, then, turns the reader's attention to the universal aspect of charisms, while focusing on church offices or leaders as part of the gifts bestowed by the Holy Spirit—"apostles, prophets, evangelists, and teachers or pastor-teachers."[38] Paul instructed on particular "church ministries/offices" and their qualifications—bishops (1 Tim 3:1–7; Titus 1:7–9), elders (1 Tim 5:17–22), deacons (1 Tim 3:8–13), and widows (1 Tim 5:3–16).[39] Garrett concludes the New Testament section with the practice of the "imposition of hands," or simply, "ordination"—Acts 6:6 (the Seven); 13:3 (Barnabas and Paul); 1 Tim 5:22 (general); and 1 Tim 4:14 and 2 Tim 1:6 (Timothy).[40]

Ordination, succinctly, is the church's public recognition and confirmation of a Christian's special "call," "charisms," and "commitment" to

34. Ibid.

35. Ibid., 2:618–19.

36. Ibid., 2:620–21. Garrett provides a historical sketch of the notion of the "Primacy of Peter and the Church of Rome" (2:514–16) and of the concept of "apostolic/episcopal succession" (2:622–24).

37. Ibid., 2:621; see also 2:222–23. Besides the Twelve and Paul (Gal 1:17; 2:8; 1 Cor 15:9), Garrett acknowledges that others were also called "apostles," such as Barnabas (Acts 14:14) and James (Gal 1:19), but he observes that the term applied in the latter case is usually translated as "messenger" (2:621; footnote 95).

38. Ibid., 2:621.

39. Ibid.

40. Ibid., 2:622.

pastoral ministry.[41] Following a Baptist heritage of the "twofold ordained ministry," Garrett seems to be supportive of the ordination only of pastors (elders, bishops, or teachers) and deacons.[42] In view of the controversial nature of the issue of "ordained women to pastoral ministry," Garrett chooses to present the principal pros and cons of the matter without stating his own position.[43] With regard to deaconship, Garrett also recognizes the controversy on "women as deacons," without, once again, disclosing his position on the matter.[44] Moreover, he points out elsewhere that the earliest General Baptist confessions of faith drawn by John Smyth (1609) and Thomas Helwys (1611) referred to men and women deacons.[45] Garrett notices that, historically and generally, deacons were responsible for the three tables—the table of the Lord (Lord's Supper), the table of the minister (pastor's need), and the table for the poor and the sick. Churches today have increasingly expected both "servant" and "ministerial" roles

41. Ibid., 2:625–26.

42. Ibid., 2:625–27, 635. Garrett observes that ordination of "church staff," who play a "supplementary" role to that of the pastor, lacks "encouragement from pastor-theologians" (2:627).

43. Ibid., 2:627–33. Not stating his position in these pages does not mean that Garrett does not take a stance regarding the ordination of women to pastoral ministry. The main arguments against women as ordained pastors include: (1) In light of the headship of man over woman in the creation order (Gen 2; 1 Cor 11:9, 12), women should be subordinate to men. (2) Because Eve was deceived by the serpent, a woman should "learn in silence" but not "teach" or "have authority" over a man (1 Tim 2:11–14). (3) Paul urged all married women not to speak in the church meetings but to "ask their own husbands at home" (1 Cor 14:33–35). (4) All of the Aaronic or Levitical priesthood established by God and the twelve apostles chosen by Jesus were males. (5) The implied "masculinity" of God and the incarnate Jesus as male suggest that the representatives of God should be males. (6) The specific qualification, "the husband of one wife" (1 Tim 3:2), indicates that only a male can be an ordained pastor.

The major arguments for women's ordination are: (1) Scripture evidences that women had "significant leadership or ministry roles" as prophetesses (e.g., Deborah—Judg 4:4; Anna—Luke 2:36; four daughters of Philip—Acts 21:9); as followers, supporters, and witnesses of Jesus (Luke 8:1–3; 24:1–11); as *diakonos* (e.g., Phoebe—Rom 16:1); and as Paul's fellow workers (e.g., Priscilla—Rom 16:3; Syntyche—Phil 4:2–3). (2) According to Galatians 3:28, all Christians are spiritually equal so that women, like men, should pastor, preach, make disciples, and minister. (3) Churches should not continuously disregard the sovereignty of the Spirit to gift (1 Cor 12:11) and to call women to "preaching-pastoral ministry." (4) History past and present shows that women pastors have served as effectively as, if not more so than, male pastors. (5) To exclude women from preaching-pastoral ministry is to leave many charisms unused.

44. Ibid., 2:635–36, for the pros and cons of women deaconship.

45. Garrett, "Professor Examines Historical Role of Deacons," August 14, 1991, 4.

in deacons—"deacons are to engage in proclamation, care-giving, and leadership," duties that "parallel those of the pastor."[46] According to Garrett, the "purpose of the deaconship," contingent upon the contexts and needs of different congregations, may involve, for example, overseeing the church's physical affairs and leading the congregation, especially in the absence of a pastor; serving in evangelism, discipleship, and care, while having other church staff or professional leaders deal with church's physical affairs; or assigning all deacons to all of the various physical and spiritual matters, including the "spiritual and emotional support for the pastor and church staff."[47]

EVALUATION OF GARRETT'S "MINISTRY" THEME

As this writer reviews Garrett's works on the Christian priesthood for ministry, three concerns become noticeable and deserve closer examination: (1) the communal nature of the priesthood as distinguished from the doctrine of "private access to God"; (2) the relation between the priesthood of all believers and the ministry of the specially called; and (3) the role of women in ordained or leadership ministry. This section attempts to evaluate these three ministry issues by comparing and contrasting Garrett's works with those of Küng, Shurden, Grenz, and Dockery, paying close attention to the aspects of communal-mutual service, universal-diversified unity, and equal-complementary ministry.

Communal and Mutual Servanthood

While agreeing that the universal priesthood is founded on God's covenant of choosing a specific people and, subsequently, embracing all believers to be a kingly-priestly people (Exod 19:6; Isa 61:6; 1 Pet 2:5, 9), Garrett and Küng concur, more significantly, that the high priesthood of Christ, though distinctly unique, is the bedrock of the identity and role of the Christian priesthood.[48] The Aaronic and Levitical priesthood has been satisfied and superseded by the high priesthood of Jesus. As Küng states forcefully, "[A]ll human priesthood has been fulfilled and finished by the unique, final, unrepeatable and hence unlimited sacrifice of the one

---

46. Garrett, *Systematic Theology*, 2:634; idem, "Professor Examines Historical Role of Deacons," August 21, 1991, 4.

47. Garrett, "Professor Examines," August 21, 1991, 4.

48. Küng, *Church*, 465–73.

continuing and eternal high priest."[49] Jesus is the perfect, sinless, unique high priest, the only irrefutable and irreplaceable mediator who opens up human access to the heavenly and holy Father; therefore, the church needs not to establish a priestly office or mediators. Both Küng and Garrett observe that the term "priests" in the New Testament is neither applied to the original twelve apostles, nor used for certain church leaders, nor listed as one of the spiritual gifts, but is reserved distinctively for Christians.[50] "Through Christ" (Heb 13:15), not by their own strength or merit, all Christians function as Christ's "ambassadors" (2 Cor 5:18–20) and as *fellow* "priests" to offer up spiritual sacrifices in the "act of witness," "confession of faith," and "service of love," in contrast to religious or ritual sacrifices.[51]

Irrefutably, the Christian priesthood is Christ-based; both Küng and Garrett attempt to demonstrate how Christians should concretely participate in the priestly ministry inaugurated by Christ. Küng, on the one hand, gives prominence to the "direct access" to God, the immediate communication with God, or the uninterrupted fellowship with God as the "ultimate freedom" and "ultimate responsibility" of every individual Christian.[52] The doctrine of "direct access," however, according to Garrett, is not the primary feature of the Christian priesthood but the corollary of Christ's priesthood (Heb 4:14–16).[53] On the other hand, Küng further argues, in view of the universal priesthood, the entire church and *every Christian* are empowered to administer baptism, the Lord's Supper, and absolution (Matt 28:19; 18:18).[54] At first glance, Küng seems to incline toward emphasizing the right and responsibility of an individual Christian-priest, and yet he intentionally cautions that recognizing "this fundamental right and duty to take an active part in baptism, the Lord's Supper and the forgiving of sins is not of course the same thing as determining who can and may be responsible for administering these sacraments in and for the community."[55] This decision, indicates Küng, belongs to the Christian

---

49. Ibid., 469.
50. Ibid., 488–89; Garrett, *Systematic Theology*, 2:609.
51. Küng, *Church*, 472–73; emphasis added.
52. Ibid., 476–77.
53. Garrett, *Systematic Theology*, 2:611, 615–16.
54. Küng, *Church*, 485–86; emphasis added.
55. Ibid., 486.

congregation as a whole.[56] Every individual priest functions within the corporate priesthood of the entire church. In general, Garrett and Küng affirm the communal responsibility of the entire Christian congregation as God's royal priesthood to fulfill the commands of Christ.

Despite the fact that Küng and Garrett apparently disagree upon whether "direct access" is the essential aspect of the Christian priesthood, they both recognize that all believers as fellow priests are called to offer "spiritual sacrifices" concretely in the forms of prayer, praise, service, self-sacrifice, and preaching.[57] Like Garrett, Küng seeks a biblical balance between "witness of actions" (i.e., loving service, good conduct) and "witness of the word" (i.e., proclamation, preaching) for the sake of fellow believers and fellow people—nonbelievers (1 Pet 2:9; 3:15; Heb 13:15).[58] The heart of the matter, as in harmony between Küng and Garrett, is that the whole community of Christians is responsible to participate actively in the priestly functions, one way or another, to reach out to fellow believers for the sake of their edification and to fellow people for the sake of their salvation. As a case in point, pertaining to preaching vis-à-vis the priesthood of believers, Küng valiantly calls attention to lay preaching and lay theologizing/teaching: "The Christian message . . . was proclaimed by all, according to their gifts and opportunities, and not just by a few with a special commission."[59] All Christians, who are "filled," "anointed," and "taught" by the Holy Spirit of the Word of God, ought to proclaim and to teach the Word of God.[60] While all believers are called to preach and teach "in the sense of their personal Christian witness" or personal testimonies to their faith in Christ, one should also recognize that, in view of the "charisms given by the Spirit," only some are specially called to be preachers and theologians for the churches.[61]

---

56. Ibid., 514–15. Küng incisively observes that Paul could have written to a particular group of leaders or officials to tell them be responsible for the issues in the church of Corinth, but he did not do so. Rather, he held the entire congregation to be responsible for the matters of immorality, discipline, preaching, and the Lord's Supper. "No one," but the whole church, "carried an exclusive responsibility for all the rest" (515).

57. Ibid., 478.

58. Ibid., 479, 486–87.

59. Ibid., 480.

60. Ibid., 480–81.

61. Ibid., 481, 483–85.

Under closer scrutiny, three interrelated aspects become particularly evident in the writings of both Küng and of Garrett concerning the believers' priesthood. First, *diakonia* or "servanthood" is essential for the priesthood doctrine. Garrett perceives that "servanthood" is Christ's primary pattern for all believers-priests—general servanthood as expressed tangibly in acts of witness, worship, stewardship, and service for the sake of the church and the community. Küng applies *diakonia* to any action or charisma empowered by the Spirit and used for the edification and the benefit of others.[62] Jesus, whose life and death were permeated with service for others (Mark 10:45; Matt 20:28), demanded his followers to do the same (John 12:25); therefore, *diakonia*, as repeatedly and rightly stressed by Küng, is the essential "characteristic," "element," and "basis" of discipleship.[63] Stated concisely, the royal priesthood is inherently *servant discipleship*.

Second, the servant-ministry of the church is vitally connected to charisms given by the Spirit. Garrett succinctly points out that the Spirit sovereignly endows and entrusts varieties of gifts to all, though different, believers "within and for the church" so that they may in turn enrich, encourage, equip, and edify one another for the "common good" (1 Cor 12:7; Eph 4:12).[64] In a similar vein, Küng articulates meticulously, "Charisma leads to diakonia since every charisma in the Church only finds fulfillment in service. Where there is real charisma, there will be responsible service for the edification and benefit of the community."[65] A charism given to each individual Christian is not intended for self-benefit, self-edification, or self-indulgence, but rather self-sacrifice on behalf of others. To each believer is given Spirit-gift(s) for loving service toward all believers, the entire body of Christ. The Christian priesthood is distinctively a *charismatic fellowship*.

Finally, charisms for mutual service, according to both Garrett and Küng, embrace church leadership—the pastoral office or ordained ministry. Church leaders and priestly believers are not oxymoronic in terms. The church officials are specially called by God, gifted by the Spirit, and recognized by the body of Christ to serve the church. Regardless of the

---

62. Ibid., 502.
63. Ibid., 499, 500, 501.
64. Garrett, *Systematic Theology*, 2:218.
65. Küng, *Church*, 502.

evident correspondence and discrepancy between the views of Küng and Garrett with regard to the completeness and categorization of charisms mentioned in Scripture (1 Cor 12:8–10; 12:28–30; Rom 12:6–8; Eph 4:11; 1 Pet 4:10–11),[66] they coincide in the conviction that charisms "are not reserved for an elitist group" but are bestowed on every believer; each and every charism is "distributed not on one's own behalf, but on behalf of others; it is . . . a call to service."[67] Church leaders or officials are no more and no less important than other Christians who are fellow servants of Christ. Put otherwise, the specially ordained ministry within the universal priesthood is essentially *servant leadership*.

Garrett emphatically points out that the terms "priests" or "priesthood" in the pertinent passages (1 Pet 2:4–10; Rev 1:5–6; 5:9–10) never appear in the singular but only in the plural.[68] He, therefore, challenges the individualistic interpretation that "every Christian is his own priest"; instead, he argues that "the apostles obviously understood the priesthood of all believers to have some corporate significance"—all Christians are priests to one another.[69] By placing Garrett and Küng in interaction with one another pertaining to the similarities and differences of their views on the priesthood doctrine, one may come to a better and deeper appreciation of Garrett's core concern with the essential character of the priesthood of believers—communal and mutual responsibility of service as captured in the concepts of "servant discipleship," "charismatic fellowship," and "servant leadership," in contrast to individual access, benefits, and rights.

Universal and Diversified Unity

When Garrett entitles the section: "General, or Lay, Ministry: Priesthood of All Christians," he unquestionably sees the doctrine of the Christian

---

66. As to completeness, neither Garrett nor Küng takes the "charism" list as comprehensive. As to categorization, Garrett does not distinctly offer his own classification, while Küng arranges charisms into three categories: "preaching"—including apostles, prophets, teachers, evangelists, and exhorters; "service"—including deacons and deaconesses who care for the needy; and "leadership"—including elders, bishops, and pastors. See Küng, *Church*, 242–43; Garrett, *Systematic Theology*, 2:218, 226.

67. Garrett, *Systematic Theology*, 2:221; Küng, *Church*, 243.

68. Garrett, *Systematic Theology*, 2:609; idem, "Biblical Doctrine of the Priesthood," 146–47.

69. Garrett, "Priesthood of All Believers," 4.

priesthood as the foundation of general church ministry; however, when he comes to the section on "Special, or Ordained, Ministry," Garrett, whether intentionally or unintentionally, seems to leave ambiguous the relation between the priesthood of all believers and the ministry of the specially called.[70] Undoubtedly, the priesthood doctrine, for Garrett, is the root of the ordained ministry; however, the question to be examined is how Garrett perceives the connection between the two. Put more plainly, "What is the precise relationship between the ordained ministry and the lay ministry?" or "What are the functions of the ordained minister vis-à-vis those of the universal priesthood?"

To answer the first question, one needs to look closely at the arguments presented by Garrett concerning the scope and nature of the priesthood of all believers. When he examines the doctrine, Garrett distinctively calls attention to the biblical lists on charisms and church leadership:

> [A]n examination of the lists of "spiritual gifts" (*charismata*) given by Paul (Rom. 12: 4–8, 1 Cor. 12: 4–11, 27–31; Eph. 4: 7–14) and of the lists of qualifications for church leaders in the Pastoral Epistles (1 Tim. 3:1–13; 5:3–22; Tit. 1:6–9) leads to the conclusion that nowhere in the New Testament is the term "priest" used to refer to a charismatic gift or a role of leadership that belongs to certain Christians but not to all Christians.[71]

Because of the absence of the term "priests" in the lists of charisms and of church leadership, the "priesthood" in the New Testament, accordingly, should not be restricted to a few but is common to all—all Christians are priests and vice versa. The universality of the Christian priesthood, in Garrett's statement above, does *not* make the ecclesial office and charisms mutually exclusive.

Noticeably in Garrett's writing, the concept of "charisma" becomes a credible clue for and a crucial connection between the priesthood of the laity and the leadership. Although the topic of spiritual gifts is discussed under the doctrine of the Holy Spirit, Garrett is aware that the Spirit-given gifts have a definite "bearing on the ministry of the churches"—the general and special ministries.[72] The intimate relation between the spiri-

---

70. Garrett, *Systematic Theology*, 2:604, 618.
71. Ibid., 2:609.
72. Ibid., 2:603. See "Holy Spirit and Spiritual Gifts" (2:215–38).

tual gifts and the Christian ministry is undeniable, particularly, in the essence of universality. Garrett would agree with the observation made by Shurden concerning the universality of charisms:

> Scholars may debate . . . whether spiritual gifts are natural talents intensified by the Holy Spirit or supernatural gifts that accompany conversion. Few would deny, however, that every Christian is endowed with a talent or ability to be used in the cause of Christ. Christian ministry cannot be restricted to religious professionals because spiritual gifts are not so confined.[73]

The actuality of the universal ministry is vitally connected to the reality of the universal charisms. The concept of "the priesthood of all believers," underscoring all believers' responsibility to serve mutually, presupposes that all believers are given charisms for such mutual service. Teaching the universal priesthood of ministry without affirming the universality of gifts to all believers is tantamount to speaking about the abstract and the ideal, but without specific capability and action. The giving of charisms is the creative and gracious way of the Trinity (1 Cor 12:4–6), who enables all believers to fulfill mutually the call to the universal priesthood.[74]

Both Garrett and Shurden acknowledge that charisms are not only universalized—to all believers, but also diversified—all believers having differing gifts (1 Cor 12:4–5; Rom 12:6).[75] These varieties of charisms unequivocally include ecclesial officers. As Garrett observes, "In two of Paul's four lists of spiritual gifts (1 Cor. 12:28; Eph. 4:11) the gifts listed are *capable of being associated with* church offices: apostles, prophets, evangelists, and teachers or pastor-teachers."[76] Immediately after establishing the definite relation between the universal charisms and special offices, Garrett further indicates that other "church ministries/offices"—bishops, deacons, elders, and widows—were also part of the charisms.[77] Adding these church offices to the lists of the spiritual gifts is not inconsistent

---

73. Shurden, *Doctrine of the Priesthood*, 99; see Garrett, *Systematic Theology*, 2:218.

74. Muthiah indicates that the priesthood doctrine grounded in the works of the Trinity, especially the diverse and yet unitive charisms of the Spirit, fosters individual responsibility or accountability, rather than arbitrariness or aloofness, in the midst of and on behalf of the congregation (Muthiah, *Priesthood of All Believers*, 68–71, 118, 119).

75. Shurden, *Doctrine of the Priesthood*, 100; Garrett, *Systematic Theology*, 2:218.

76. Garrett, *Systematic Theology*, 2:621; emphasis added.

77. Ibid., 2:621.

for Garrett, since the Pauline lists "should not be taken as exhaustive or complete."[78] In this line of reasoning, Garrett has no difficulty arguing that the office of deacons, as well as that of pastors-elders-bishops, is none other than a Spirit-given gift.[79]

Universality of charisms does not denote *uniformity* of all believers; *diversity* of the gifts does not mean *division* in the church. Rather, as Garrett states distinctly,

> [T]he Spirit bestows the various gifts within and for the church. Such giving is "for the common good" . . . (1 Cor. 12: 7). By analogy, the parts of the human body are to have "the same care" . . . or "the same concern" . . . [or] "for one another" (1 Cor. 12:25b). The gifts are given "to equip the saints for the work of ministry, for building up the body of Christ" (Eph. 4:12).[80]

The diversity of gifts should result in unity, mutuality, and maturity of the body of Christ, instead of discord, detachment, and deformity. Shurden, speaking in the same vein, indicates that when the church "uniforms" the gifts, the result is deformity, dearth, and even demise of the church: "This variety of gifting by God is no act of divine caprice . . . Conformity deforms. Diversity gives life . . . Diverse gifts distributed to all priests work together to create the whole."[81] One's gift is not the entirety. The truth of diversity teaches that the church should neither "underestimate" and "underemploy" the gifts among the laity nor overemphasize and "overwork" the gifts of, for example, the ecclesial offices.[82] Shurden states pointedly, "We are priests to one another, and our gifts are 'for the common good.'"[83] Garrett and Shurden generally reach a positive rapport with respect to the universality and diversity of the charisms vis-à-vis the mutuality of the universal priesthood. The Spirit sovereignly bestows diversified charisms on believers universally so that the entire Christian priesthood, whether laity or leadership, is able to reach the unity and

---

78. Ibid., 2:218.

79. Garrett observes that that the original charisma of service (*diakonia*) gradually developed into the office of deacons (*diakonos*) in the New Testament (ibid., 2:631). Garrett comments on Acts 20:17–35 that the terms "bishop," "pastors," and "elders" are "differing functions for the same persons, not three different offices" (2:625).

80. Ibid., 2:218.

81. Shurden, *Doctrine of the Priesthood*, 100, 101, 102.

82. Ibid., 102, 105.

83. Ibid., 104.

maturity of the body of Christ, resulting in edifying the church mutually and glorifying God ultimately (1 Pet 4:10–11).

Since the special ministry is part of the divinely universal and diversified gifts to the priesthood of all believers, what exactly should the called or ordained leaders do? Are their functions distinct from those of the general priesthood, as expressed in witness, worship, stewardship, and service? As aforementioned, the prophetic, princely, and priestly function of Christ is the focal point for the special ministry as well as for the general ministry.[84] Concisely, the mission of the "Servant of the Lord" (Matt 12:17–21; Isa 42:1–4) fulfilled in self-sacrificial service was Jesus' central ministry (Mark 10:45; Luke 22:27). Jesus expected his disciples' "followship" to be characterized by the corresponding "servanthood" (John 12:20–26). In terms of the believers' priesthood, the function of the specially-called is not distinct from that of the corporate priesthood—servant-ministry. In this sense, the body of believers constitutes a fellowship of Christian priests serving one another.

On the other hand, Jesus specially called the twelve disciples to "exercise special functions"—"teaching, preaching, and healing" (Matt 9:35—11:1); a "witness to Jesus' resurrection" (Acts 1:22); and the "ministry of the word" with prayer (Acts 6:4).[85] Despite his view on the cessation of the apostolic office, Garrett is convinced that God continuously calls and gifts certain Christians to exercise pastoral, preaching, teaching, and leadership functions—pastors and deacons—within and for the church; therefore, Christian congregations should be ready to recognize and ratify, by means of ordination, such special callings and charisms.[86] Garrett's reference to Luther's view on the ordained ministry may be an adequate recapitulation of Garrett's own view: "For Luther, the called, ordained ministry is both derivative from the priesthood of all Christians and something directly instituted by Jesus Christ, and the call is both inner (from God) and outer (through men)."[87] It is a fair assessment or statement that, for Garrett, the universal priesthood of all Christians and the special commission of Christ in the context of the church constitute the ordained ministry.

---

84. Garrett, *Systematic Theology*, 2:618, 620.
85. Ibid., 2:620.
86. Ibid., 2:218, 625–26.
87. Ibid., 2:624.

What are the specific functions of the specially called or ordained ministries—pastorate and deaconship—in relation to the priesthood of all believers? Garrett does not give an answer forthrightly, but his writing provides certain indications of the roles of the ordained ministries. The pastor's primary function involves "preaching," "teaching," "shepherding," and "leading."[88] The roles of deacons (*diakonos*) basically pertain to *diakonia*, which involves service—physical or spiritual—to the poor, the people, and the pastor.[89] In a general sense, all believers are *called* to proclaim by words and to serve by deeds; in a narrow sense, however, only some are specially *called and gifted* to commit to the roles of preaching, teaching, and reaching. Such calling and charisma are recognized by the local congregation by means of ordination.

Since Garrett sees the ecclesial offices as being part of the charisms, which he regards as the basic connection between the general and special ministries of the church, the ultimate aims of the ecclesial offices (pastors and deacons), from a "charisms" perspective, are not distinct from but united with those of other ministries—that is, they are given for benefiting others (1 Cor 12:7, 25b), for edifying the church (Eph 4:12), and for glorifying God (1 Pet 4:11). Shurden likewise, speaking from the vantage point of "charisma," states that the special or ordained ministry is one function or gift among many, and yet it serves to "facilitate the ministry of the church."[90] Based on Ephesians 4:11–12,[91] Shurden explains that the ordained ministers are supposed to "prepare," "equip," or "furnish" all believers to participate in the mission and ministry of the church. Ordained ministries "facilitate the total ministry of the church"; that is, they have an "equipping ministry."[92] Realistically, Shurden urges that as equippers ordained ministers should themselves be equipped adequately and con-

---

88. Ibid., 2:625, 633. In his most recent essay, Garrett clearly states, "The pastor is to preach/teach, engage in pastoral care, and lead in church administration." (Garrett, "Under the Lordship of Christ through Democratic Processes," 126).

89. Garrett, *Systematic Theology*, 2:634–35.

90. Shurden, *Doctrine of the Priesthood*, 105.

91. "And He gave some as apostles, and some as prophets, and some as evangelists, and some as pastors and teachers, for the equipping of the saints for the work of service, to the building up of the body of Christ."

92. Shurden, *Doctrine of the Priesthood*, 107–8. Garrett notes, "The gifted leaders were given 'to prepare the Lord's people for works of service, so that the body of Christ may be built up until we all reach unity in the faith and in the knowledge of the Son of God and become mature'" (Garrett, "Congregation-Led Church," 186).

tinuously. Practically, he recommends that ecclesial officials should at least "identify gifts of other priests," "specify needs of ministry," and "motivate through teaching/preaching." By being equipped constantly and by equipping others consistently, the ordained ministers will be less likely to encounter ministerial "rustout" and "burnout."[93] Garrett is not unaware of the overloaded and overworked ministers trying to meet the "many demands" and "high expectation" of their congregations.[94] To transform the situation, Garrett, in principle, resonates with Shurden in contending that the general and special ministries, under the common rubric of the universal priesthood, should seek to serve mutually for the one unitive purpose of "building up the body of Christ," which eventually results in the glory of God.[95]

To recapitulate, using the crucial clue of "charisma" in Garrett's writing as a frame of reference, one is able to discern the vital connection between the priesthood of general ministry and that of the special ministry. The functions of the laity and the leadership are as universal and diverse as the charisms, but they have the united vision and mission of serving others mutually so that the entire church may be built up for the glory of God, which is precisely the primary function of the priesthood of all believers.

Equal and Complementary Ministry

One subject that remains to be analyzed within Garrett's priesthood doctrine concerns gender roles in ministry: "Can women be ordained ministers of the church?" Garrett does not disclose his own position on this matter. By means of interacting with selected contemporary theologians, particularly Grenz and Dockery, who have dealt with the question of women roles in ministry, this section attempts a twofold task: (1) to explore two basic characters of the Christian priesthood in relation to gender roles—the concepts of *equality* and *complementarity* in ministry; and (2) to draw a logical and plausible conclusion regarding Garrett's view on the role of women in ministry as it relates to his doctrine of the believers' priesthood.

---

93. Shurden, *Doctrine of the Priesthood*, 108–9.
94. Garrett, *Systematic Theology*, 2:633.
95. See Garrett, "Under the Lordship," 127.

Kärkkäinen perhaps rightly comments that the Free churches and believers' churches put into practice the priesthood doctrine, emphasizing the "gifting of each believer for ministry as *equal* partners ... Members of the church, including women with little and no education, have had the opportunity to participate in all kinds of service in the church."[96] Thus far, Garrett's concept of the universal priesthood urges the opening of church ministry to all believers; all, both men and women, are called and gifted to participate in the church's ministry. In like manner, Christian theologians who advocate the priesthood doctrine embrace the equality of men and women in Christian ministry. Despite diversity of functions, declares Shurden, the believers' priesthood implies no clerical hierarchy but equal fellowship.[97] Muthiah contends that all charisms are "marked by an equality of value" as the "Trinity is marked by equality"; therefore, no Christian-priest "within this royal priesthood is more important than any of the other priests."[98] Kärkkäinen calls for an "egalitarian model of the church where all persons, regardless of their status (ordained and non-ordained) and gender, are given an opportunity to serve through their manifold gifts"; in other words, the Spirit's "universal distribution" of the gifts "makes all the members of the church equal."[99] To Ogden, "[T]he clearest expression of body ministry's becoming a reality has been the influx of able and gifted women into service . . . [A]ll God's people are ministers."[100] In short, by virtue of the indwelling and enabling of the Spirit, the aspect of equality—ontological equality in Christ or impartial opportunities to serve in ministry—seems to be self-evident in the doctrine of the priesthood of all believers.

Other theologians, who also support the characteristic of equality in the priesthood doctrine, clearly express that women should not be prohibited from preaching, teaching, leadership, or the pastoral role. Küng, in view of universal charisms within the priesthood of all believers, asserts that there is no "dogmatic ground" to prohibit women from preaching and teaching.[101] By the same token, Grenz avers that denying women

---

96. Kärkkäinen, *Introduction to Ecclesiology*, 65–66; emphasis added.
97. Shurden, *Doctrine of the Priesthood*, 68.
98. Muthiah, *Priesthood of All Believers*, 72–73.
99. Kärkkäinen, "Calling of the People of God into Ministry," 145, 152.
100. Ogden, *Unfinished Business*, 34.
101. Küng, *Church*, 483–84.

from serving in ordained or pastoral leadership is to make irrelevant the doctrine of the priesthood of all believers that opens the door of ministry to all.[102] Grenz argues, "Because Christ has qualified all believers to stand in God's presence, regardless of race, social status or gender, we are all ministers . . . As priests of God . . . we are called by the Spirit to ministries . . . [which] include positions of leadership."[103] Pastoral ministry, as Grenz continues, is "an extension of the universal ministry of Christ's body" and is "charismatic in character"; therefore, it is "to be filled by persons gifted for the pastorate, whether male or female . . ."[104] Grenz reminds us of the Spirit's sovereign will to call any believer whom the Spirit has gifted for the pastoral role.[105] Grenz and Garrett seem to have two basic notions in common. First, pastoral ministry flows or derives from the universal ministry or general priesthood; therefore, both ministries are equally necessary to the church—one is not to control the other but to complement each other. Second, the pastoral office is a Spirit-given gift; therefore, the Spirit determines, as he pleases, the person to be gifted for the role. The probing question is: "If Garrett accepts the premise of the Spirit's sovereign gifting as the determinative factor for the pastoral role, could it suggest that Garrett concurs with the fact that the Spirit may call and gift a woman for pastoral ministry?" It is indeed a logical possibility but may not be the only possible answer for Garrett.

Delineating the reasoning of Dockery, who attempts to formulate a mediating view for the role of women in ministry, may help provide further insights into Garrett's stance on the role of women. In a word, Dockery holds to the ontological equality of men and women and the complementarity of men and women in ministerial functions. Dockery endeavors to identify the "normative principles" in the "didactic passages," and harmonize them with the contextual practices and commands in the "descriptive passages."[106] First, by union with Christ, all people, regardless of race, social status, or gender, enjoy "equality" or "equal partnership" (Gal 3:28). Second, Christian men and women have functional differences, a reality that is embedded in the order of creation rather than

---

102. Grenz, "Biblical Priesthood and Women in Ministry," 276.
103. Ibid.
104. Ibid., 278, 283.
105. Ibid., 286.
106. Dockery, "Role of Women," 363–86.

being a result of the fall (1 Cor 11:2–16; cf. Gen 2:18–25). Third, women may pray and prophesy (1 Cor 11:5) on the basis that they concede to the principles of submission and orderliness; otherwise, they must remain silent (1 Cor 14:34). Fourth, women may be involved in the teaching ministry but not have "the position of final authoritative public teacher in the assembly," based on the order of creation and the sequence of the fall (1 Tim 2:11–15).[107] Dockery, on the other hand, finds it difficult to deny that in the descriptive passages, "[W]omen had positions of leadership and influence in the early church . . . women could lead, minister and serve in a variety of capacities"; hence, as an attempt at harmonization, Dockery proposes:

> Women could teach, lead, minister and perhaps hold office (or at least carry out such functions) so long as it was done orderly and modestly (1 Cor 11:2–16; 14:40), so long as leadership was not usurped in public meetings (1 Tim 2:11–15), and so long as women did not exercise authority over men in matters of church administration and teaching (1 Tim 2:11–15 and 1 Cor 14:33–35).[108]

By implication, these principles disallow the ordination of women for ministry positions that "include authority in matters of teaching and administration, but not for positions that include serving or diaconal functions."[109] Dockery concludes and urges that the attention should not be on ordination but on the "gifts and functions of ministry" of both men and women to meet the "present needs and situations" of the church, to "magnify Jesus Christ, the head of the church," and to "enhance the propagation of the gospel."[110]

Like Dockery, Garrett is fully cognizant of both the "didactic passages" against women's ordination to the pastoral office and the "descriptive passages" supporting women as ministers.[111] To deny either outright runs the risk of disregarding the underlying principles or their historical contexts relevant to women's role in ministry. A plausible alternative for Garrett seems to be assuming a harmonic position which neither violates

---

107. Ibid., 366, 368, 370, 372–73.

108. Ibid., 375.

109. Ibid., 385.

110. Ibid., 385–86. Dockery gives a compelling example of Mrs. W. A. Criswell, who was a gifted Bible teacher of the First Baptist Church of Dallas, TX, and taught "a large influential class of men and women" (385, footnote 72).

111. Garrett, *Systematic Theology*, 2:630.

the integrity of the text-contexts nor neglects the biblical principle of the universal priesthood. In his writing, Garrett, in fact, concludes the pros-and-cons debates on the ordination of women by pointing out two contemporary examples of mediating postures without, of course, indicating whether any of those is his preference—first, by encouraging women to serve in any ministerial capacity (e.g., deacons, Sunday School teachers), except the teaching-ruling office; second, by redefining "laying on of hands" or "ordination" to mean "induction into service rather than bestowal of authority."[112]

By comparison, both Garrett and Dockery acknowledge the equality of men and women—all are equal in Christ; all are called to serve according to their giftedness, regardless of their gender; they are equal partners in ministry. The Spirit gives charisms to all Christians, the reality that underscores the universality of the charisms and the ontological equality of all believers. On the other hand, Christians are *not* equally gifted or are gifted differently, a truth that highlights the diversified and complementary functionality of all believers. Concisely, equal partnership and complementary service in ministry are the essential characteristics of the priesthood of all believers.

Garrett and Dockery appear to be in agreement that women may be ordained deacons or, at the least, qualified to carry out the *diakonal* function. Deaconship, by definition, is a gift of *diakonia* (serving function), and the ordination of a deacon is a congregational recognition and confirmation of one's calling and charisma rather than a bestowal of authority to be an authoritative public teacher in the church.[113] The key question should be, "Could Garrett's principle of the universal priesthood embrace the idea that all believers are gifted to serve one another in various capacities but allow only men to be called to the final authoritative role—leader-pastor-teacher—of the church?" This is a plausible option for Garrett.

Corporate servanthood, communal mutuality, and complementary equality in ministry characterize Garrett's priesthood doctrine; all Christians are fellow priests who are bestowed with diversified gifts to serve each other. The ordained pastorate, though a leadership position, is part of the charisms given for serving the body of Christ. Garrett would

---

112. Ibid., 2:632–33.
113. Dockery, "Role of Women in Worship and Ministry," 385.

not deny that, normatively, Christian men ought to be the authoritative leaders, teachers, or pastors, according to the principles of headship and the order of creation. Garrett would concede that women should actively be involved in various church ministries, in accordance with the variety of charisms and with the principle of submission. Diversity of gifts and submission to authority are not inconsistent with ontological equality in Christ;[114] they imply functional mutuality and complementarity. Having said that, in line with his priesthood doctrine in the framework of the Spirit's sovereign giving of charisms, Garrett would not deny that God, on exceptional occasions, may call and gift certain women for leadership or a pastoral position.

"Can women be ordained pastors of the church?" Mohler called this the "second-order issue" that "would prevent two Christians from joining the same covenant community, even though they would still call one another 'Christians.'"[115] Garrett does not disclose his distinct stance on the issue in his writing. He only provides arguments from the two opposing camps as well as a couple of mediating alternatives. On the one hand, Garrett in this respect shows his irenic spirit in his theological work; but on the other hand, it becomes difficult, though not impossible, for anyone to attempt to determine his view on women's ordination. One aspect is certain—that Garrett aspires to show that Christian ministry rooted in the priesthood doctrine involves the entire participation of the Christian members in mutual servanthood, according to their giftedness, to build up the body of Christ. Garrett's intentional obscurity of his personal conviction in the matter of women's ordination may as well be his message to the churches that rather than battling over the issue, the crucial concern is, borrowing Dockery's words, to "seek to determine what gifts women have and how they can be effective in worship and ministry opportunities."[116] This summary statement fundamentally resonates with the essence of Garrett's doctrine of the universal ministry of all believers.

CONCLUSION

By reviewing the priesthood of Christ, the priesthood of all believers, and the priesthood of the ordained ministry in Garrett's ministry theme, three

114. Grudem, "Wives Like Sarah, and the Husbands Who Honor Them," 195–96.
115. Mohler, "Southern Baptist Identity," 31.
116. Dockery, "Role of Women," 385.

issues emerge to become the subjects of this writer's investigation—mutual service versus private status; ministry of the people and ministry of the ordained; and the issue of women's ordination in ministry. In the process of evaluating these main concerns, the chapter shows that Garrett's view of the ministry is consistently rooted in the character of the priesthood of all believers: first, *communal-mutual servanthood*—all believers, including the ordained ministers, are fellow servants, who serve according to their charisms, rather than private priests who demand individualistic privileges, a problem often issuing from the doctrine of "direct access"; second, *universal-diversified unity*—the general and special ministries are essentially derived from the same source, the doctrine of the believers' priesthood, which in turn is grounded in the priesthood of Christ. Both ministries are one in unity because they are charisms given by the sovereign Spirit to all believers, universally and diversely, so the body of Christ can reach mutuality, unity, and maturity; and third, *equal-complementary ministry*—while Garrett does not explicitly disclose his personal posture toward the women's ordination issue, his intention is not to create a sense of mystery on his part, but to motivate all Christians, especially women, to active ministry. Garrett definitively does not aspire to create division among churches merely because of raising the issues of women's ordination. Instead, he simply encourages complementarity among Christian members—both men and women—on the basis that all are equally fellow priests in servanthood for the edification of the church and glory of God.

chapter 5

The Management of the Church

INTRODUCTION

THE OBJECTIVE OF THIS chapter is to show that Garrett's writings on the theme of church management reflect a distinct and direct application of his doctrine of the Christian priesthood. The first section provides a selective and succinct review of Garrett's works pertaining to ecclesial governance—"Church–State Relations," "Congregation Polity," and "Church Discipline." The second main section will provide an in-depth assessment of the three subjects in juxtaposition with the pertinent ecclesial perspectives of three other theologians—Malcolm B. Yarnell (Baptist), John H. Yoder (Mennonite), and Avery Dulles (Roman Catholic)—to elucidate Garrett's recurrent ideas of corporate authority, congregational participation, and communal discipleship.

CHURCH-STATE RELATIONS

According to Garrett, Baptists express their doctrine of the universal priesthood in two major forms: believer's baptism and religious liberty.[1] Religious liberty or freedom undeniably has a bearing upon the issue of church-and-state relations or separation, an issue integrally linked to that of religious authority.[2]

---

1. Garrett, *Systematic Theology*, 2:614. For a detailed discussion of believer's baptism, see chapter 3, "The Membership of the Church."

2. Garrett observes a fine distinction between religious liberty and church-state

By expounding Romans 13:1–7, Garrett shows that Christians are obliged by conscience to render "obedient submission to the governing authorities of the civil state," such as paying taxes and showing respect to the authorities, because the latter are the divinely ordained institutions for peace and order of the society.[3] In view of Revelation 13, however, if the civil state at any point in time, "authorized and empowered by Satan," commits "blasphemy and/or idolatry" by expecting "worship" from its citizens and by persecuting churches, Christians ought to resist obeying the civil state as the "highest governing authorities." Even in the face of "social ostracism," "economic persecution," "imprisonment, and/or death," Christians are also urged to persist under political persecution with "loyalty, courage, and faithfulness" to God.[4] Christians have a "dual" and "dialectic" mandate: to be subject to human authorities (Rom 13:1) and to obey God (Acts 5:29).[5] Nevertheless, Christians' "loyalty to God and to Caesar [human government] is not a 50-50 matter; rather, loyalty to God is primary and ultimate," explains Garrett.[6]

Jesus and his disciples practiced religious freedom—they "persuaded" rather than persecuted; they employed "verbal" rather than "violent" means; they were "prophetic" rather than "coercive."[7] Garrett states affirmatively,

> Religious freedom is consistent with the biblical concepts of man's answerability to God; of faith as persuasion; of the suffering of Jesus as the Messiah; of the church as a gathered, witnessing, ser-

---

separation: "Whereas historically the advocacy of religious liberty was one major factor contributing to the framing of national constitutions prescribing church-state separation and whereas practically religious liberty usually suffers when either one church dominates the state or the state dominates the churches, religious liberty to a considerably high degree may exist even where established churches still survive." Garrett, "Religious Liberty, Vatican Council II, and Baptists," 175.

3. Garrett, "Dialectic of Romans 13:1–7 and Revelation 13: Part One," 441–42.
4. Garrett, "Dialectic of Romans 13:1–7 and Revelation 13: Part Two," 20.
5. Garrett, "Religious Freedom: Church and State," 10.
6. Garrett, *Systematic Theology*, 2:693.
7. Garrett, "Religious Freedom: Why and How in Today's World," 10–11. Garrett observes that some "modern scholars [attempted] to establish the thesis that Jesus was a Zealot and hence a violent revolutionary. This thesis has been effectively refuted by other scholars who have demonstrated the essentially nonviolent and non-revolutionary nature of Jesus' mission and activity" (Garrett, *Systematic Theology*, 2:691–92).

vant community; of the limits to the competence of the state; and of the lordship of Christ and the sovereignty of God.[8]

In particular, the "lordship of Christ" or the "sovereignty of God" means the ultimate, divine, and direct authority over the universe, particularly over churches and Christians. Since Christians confess their "ultimate allegiance" to the lordship of Christ, when a civil state "usurps the authority that rightly belongs to the exalted Son of God, that state is guilty of blasphemy," warns Garrett.[9] Thus, religious freedom entails "institutional separation of church and state," which includes "disestablishment" or no establishment of a state church as well as no inherently necessary cooperation between civil governments and Christ's churches.[10] It is, however, a moot point whether or not Scripture speaks unequivocally on the issues of Christian participation in public office, military service, warfare, or revolution against the civil state,[11] but Garrett clearly urges that, in the matter of church-state relations, churches "need to continue to reassess their diaconal responsibilities and priorities,"[12] the ministerial functions which are nothing less than "proclamation, witness, service, and self-giving love."[13]

CONGREGATIONAL POLITY

Writing on church polity, Garrett begins by indicating the relation between the Trinitarian identity of the church and its concrete expression of this identity in church governance:

---

8. Garrett, "Religious Freedom: Why and How," 12. For a fuller discussion of these biblical concepts, see Garrett, "Biblical Basis of Religious Liberty," 283–86.

9. Garrett, "Biblical Basis of Religious Liberty," 286.

10. Garrett, "Religious Freedom: Why and How," 20–22. Garrett identifies four major historic models of church-state relations: (1) distinct alienation/separation of church and state; (2) theocratic model—"subordination of the civil government to the prevailing church"; (3) Erastian model—"subordination of the church or churches to the civil state"; and (4) "via media" model—state established churches which functioned within the theocratic and Erastian extremes (Garrett, *Systematic Theology*, 2:702).

11. Garrett, "Dialectic of Romans 13:1–7 and Revelation 13: Part Two," 20. Garrett states: "Revelation 13 clearly identifies persecution but is silent on such issues as the holding of public office and military service by Christians, the right of revolution against tyranny, and the welfare state" (Garrett, *Systematic Theology*, 2:701).

12. Garrett, "Religious Freedom: Why and How," 22.

13. Garrett, "Biblical Basis of Religious Liberty," 285.

> If the church of Jesus Christ is to be identified as the people of God, the body of Christ, and the fellowship of the Holy Spirit, why should the methods or procedures according to which particular expressions of the church conduct their affairs and make their decisions be important? It is partly because of the very human aspect of the church as an ordered society living on the earth in a specific time period within history.[14]

The Trinitarian nature of the church (divine aspect) is not unrelated to how the church functions on earth (human aspect). *What or who the church is* directly affects and effects *what the church does and how the church behaves.* How exactly does the Trinitarian character of the church impact and illuminate the life of the congregation? Garrett notes that the "New Testament does not prescribe or mandate a detailed system of church polity" but a general "pattern" along with essential "principles" for church government.[15] He believes there is a biblical pattern of church government—congregational structure—that seemingly prevails over three other general forms—"papal," "episcopal," and "presbyterial" modes.[16]

In "The Congregation-Led Church: Congregational Polity," Garrett unapologetically argues for the congregational management of the church. For this mode of governance, the "final human authority" lies with the "local or particular congregation when it gathers for decision-making" with respect to all matters, spanning from membership to leadership, from ministration to administration, from doctrine to discipline.[17] The whole congregation is responsible to make all decisions, "except when such have been delegated by the congregation to individual members of groups or members."[18] Garrett succinctly defines "congregational polity" as the church managing itself "under the lordship of Jesus Christ (Christocracy) and with the leadership of the Holy Spirit (pneumatophoria) with no

---

14. Garrett, *Systematic Theology*, 2:639. At the outset of his ecclesiology, Garrett has already observed the significance of the Trinitarian nature of the church: "Present-day biblical scholars and theologians in various Christian denominations or confessions are demonstrating a high level of agreement in their exposition of the principal New Testament metaphors for the church"—the Trinitarian metaphors of the church (see the chart on 2:513).

15. Ibid., 2:639; idem, "Congregation-Led Church," 172.

16. For a concise review of the differing practices of polity, see Garrett, *Systematic Theology*, 2:641–45.

17. Garrett, "Congregation-Led Church," 157.

18. Ibid.

superior or governing ecclesial bodies (autonomy) and with every member having a voice in its affairs and its decisions (democracy)."[19] Within congregational polity, there are, nonetheless, differing practices ("independent" or "interdependent/cooperative posture") and various structures (pastor-deacons, or pastor-deacons-committees, or pastor-deacons-committees-church council structures), but all of which are "subject to the final authority of the congregation," maintains Garrett.[20]

Garrett identifies six supposedly direct and distinct biblical supports for congregational polity: a locally gathered Christian congregation was responsible for implementing church discipline (Matt 18:15–20); choosing the first seven deacons (Acts 6:3); commissioning Barnabas and Saul (Acts 13:2–3); selecting Judas and Silas (Acts 15:22); excommunicating the incestuous member (1 Cor 5:2); and enforcing discipline as well as forgiveness (2 Cor 2:6–8).[21] Congregational polity is not only crucially and consistently related to the exercise of spiritual gifts; the maturity, mission, and ministry of all Christian members; the implementation of church discipline; and the fulfillment of the Great Commission, but also, as Garrett indicates, is embedded foremost in the doctrine of the priesthood of all Christians, especially when congregational polity "is understood as the Congregational governance by all the believers."[22]

How to manage or govern the church of God is not a matter of personal whimsicality or cultural relativity, but a matter of biblical authority. For Garrett, the congregational polity of the church is a direct implication of the priesthood of all believers. "If all the believers are to exercise the 'royal priesthood' (1 Pet. 2:9) through the offering of various spiritual sacrifices, then why should not those same believers together participate in and be responsible for the decision-making of the congregation?" asks Garrett.[23] He is adamant about the full participation or responsibility of all believers in church life, a direct corollary of the universal priesthood.

---

19. Ibid., 158; idem, *Systematic Theology*, 2:644.

20. Garrett, "Congregation-Led Church," 158.

21. See ibid., 158–70, for detailed explanation of the passages.

22. Ibid., 184–89; esp. 185. Note that Garrett places the doctrine of the believers' priesthood first among his theological arguments for congregational polity.

23. Ibid., 185.

CHURCH DISCIPLINE

Garrett has been instrumental in recovering and reviving the most neglected and dreaded topic among Baptist churches—church discipline.[24] Using the *Summary of Church Discipline* by the Charleston Baptist Association (1773) as a stepping-stone, he urges Southern Baptist churches to practice "disciplined churchmanship."[25] Church discipline and Christian discipleship are so significantly linked that the latter has a "direct bearing on the order and ethics of the New Testament churches," both then and today.[26] Denying oneself and taking up the cross (Mark 8:34); serving and loving fellow disciples (Mark 10:43–45; John 15:12–13); and making and teaching disciples (Matt 28:19–20) are some of the major signs of discipleship or positive discipline.[27]

Garrett, then, turns the reader's attention to the negative discipline or "non-discipleship" in the New Testament, especially citing Matthew 18:15–17 and 1 Corinthians 5:9–13 pertaining to the practice and principle of congregational responsibility for excommunicating or disfellowshipping an offending, unrepentant member: "The Christian fellowship is to 'judge' those inside the church and to 'drive out' the wicked person ... from among them."[28] Whether issues relative to ethics, unity, or doctrines, the church should "decide in such matters" because "'the saints will judge the world' and even 'angels'" (1 Cor 6:2–3), states Garrett.[29]

What is the proper manner of the "renewal of disciplined discipleship"? Garrett is convinced that such renewal of discipline can best be initiated and implemented through and by Christians as a whole, who are members of the local churches.[30] Garrett denounces discipline that is "initiated and administered *solely* by the minister" as "a travesty of congregationalism."[31] He concludes perceptively,

---

24. Garrett, "Church Discipline: Lost, but Recoverable," 21. This article was originally published in *Western Recorder* (July 23, 1959).
25. Garrett, *Baptist Church Discipline*, 1.
26. Ibid., 5.
27. Ibid.
28. Ibid., 6–7.
29. Ibid., 7.
30. Ibid., 26.
31. Ibid., 27; emphasis original.

> Church discipline must be redemptive in purpose and not merely punitive. Grace and forgiveness must always be operative. The restoration of the offending brother must be of equal importance with the purity of the church. Anything less cannot be squared with our Lord and the New Testament.[32]

To summarize, a review of Garrett's "management" theme discloses three significant issues: (1) Who is responsible for the spiritual matters of the church? The church, not the civil state, holds the final accountability in all ecclesial matters. (2) How should the church direct its own life? The whole membership of the local congregation, not merely the leaders, should participate in the decision-making process of the church under the lordship of Christ with the leadership of the Spirit. (3) Why is the whole congregation responsible for deciding on all its ecclesial matters, even the matter of church discipline? The goal is to fulfill the congregational task of discipleship by producing mature and disciplined membership. The next section examines these three subjects in details.

EVALUATION OF THE "MANAGEMENT" THEME

Corporate Authority

Garrett's church "management" theme—focusing on church-state relations, congregational polity, and church discipline—converges on one patent aspect: authority. It is essentially about who has the final authority to decide or determine on the "what," "whom," and "how" of the church's life. Church-state relations primarily deal with the question of who has the decisive *authority* over the spiritual matters of the church. Congregational polity, as a direct response to the issue of church-state relations, affirms that the congregation must exercise final *authority* over ecclesial matters. Church discipline, as a direct application of congregational polity, demonstrates that the local Christian fellowship has definitive *authority* in the discipline-discipleship of its members. In short, Garrett is convinced that the local Christian congregation possesses the determinative human authority over its own congregational beliefs, practices, and members, without the intervening or interfering power of other external bodies, whether religious or political.[33]

---

32. Ibid. For a recent work on biblical church discipline, see Richardson, *Walking Together: A Congregational Reflection on Biblical Church Discipline*.

33. Garrett, "Congregation-Led Church," 158.

As he argues that the local congregation holds the *final* authority over all spiritual and ecclesial matters, Garrett concurrently recognizes a twofold and triune underpinning for such a view on congregational management. First, the living reality of the supremacy of the triune God—the "sovereignty of God," the "lordship of Christ" (Christocracy), and the "leadership of the Holy Spirit" (pneumatophoria) taken synonymously—is the sure foundation of church "autonomy" (no externally superior governing entities).[34] Second, the triune character of the church—the "people of God," the "body of Christ," and the "fellowship of the Holy Spirit"—is the ground for congregational "democracy" (all church members are equally responsible for all church decisions).[35] The church as the "people," the "body," and the "fellowship" of the triune God, on the one hand, indicates its original and authoritative source in the Trinity, and on the other hand, implies its primary character—the equality, solidarity, and communality of all Christians. A logical consequence of the supreme authority of the triune God and the Trinitarian identity of the church *is* precisely the royal priesthood of all believers, a fellowship of believers who participate in the kingly rule of God in the church.[36] The immediate and ultimate kingship of the triune God over his church demands no other external or superior authority. The Christian community—chosen by the Father, redeemed by the Son, and indwelt by the Spirit—is to govern itself under the divine authority. Thus, for Garrett, authority resides *finally* in the Christian congregation and yet *ultimately* in God.

Garrett is not alone in expounding the divine-human authority of Christ's church. Yarnell, who was under the tutelage of Garrett and is now professor of theology at Southwestern Baptist Seminary, directly addresses the much underdeveloped theme of Christian "priests and kings"—the "ruling function"—by analyzing the three passages particularly pertaining to the Christian priesthood in Revelation (1:4–8; 5:6–10; 20:4–6).[37] He

---

34. Ibid., 158; idem, "Biblical Basis of Religious Liberty," 286. Garrett states that the "early free church and Baptist foundation for religious liberty . . . was not man's autonomy, reason, or freedom, but the Lordship of Jesus in the Church and over conscience" (Garrett, "Religious Liberty, Vatican Council II, and Baptists," 185).

35. Garrett, *Systematic Theology*, 2:639; idem, "Congregation-Led Church," 158.

36. Küng argues that a "logical conclusion" about the nature of the church—the people of God, the body of Christ, and the temple of the Holy Spirit—is the doctrine of the Christian priesthood (Küng, *Church*, 473–76).

37. Yarnell, "Priesthood of Believers," 229, 243.

incisively identifies the Trinitarian theme: the Father as the one "who is and who was and who is to come" (Rev 1:4a) and "who sat on the throne" (5:1); the Spirit as "the seven Spirits who are before His thrones" (1:4b) and "the seven Spirits of God" proceeding from the Son (5:6); and Jesus Christ as "the faithful witness, the firstborn of the dead, and the ruler of the kings of the earth" (1:5), as well as the "Lion" and the "Lamb" (5:5–6), with an emphasis on Jesus, who has the *triplex munus* and who created the Christian priesthood.[38] Furthermore, Yarnell observes the past, present, and future aspects of the Christian priesthood: "In [Revelation] 1:6, Christians have been made priests; in 5:10, Christians are currently serving as a priestly kingdom before the throne of God; and, in 20:6, their kingship will come into material fullness."[39] Even though the full and visible kingship will not be realized until the *eschaton*, when Christians will reign with Jesus, Yarnell unambiguously argues for the present reality of Christian kingship in the form of congregational management under the direct kingship of Christ: "The kingdom has yet to fully come, but the church, which has Christ as its King, finds its member-kings should now participate in the eternal kingdom through congregational governance."[40] Yarnell concludes pointedly that while there is a "qualitative distinction" between the priesthood of Christ and of believers, Scripture does not imply any "qualitative distinctions . . . within the membership of the royal priesthood"; therefore, no believer-priest, whether a pastor or a layperson, stands above or under other Christians, but rather, in view of Revelation 1:6; 5:10; 1 Corinthians 5–6; and Matthew 18:15–18, all should exercise their corporate kingship by congregational governance, particularly through church discipline as a "precursor of their future exercise of judgment" (Rev 19–20).[41]

By placing Yarnell's exposition in conversation with Garrett's explication on the authority of the church of Christ, three features become discernible for further deliberation. First, the direct kingship of the triune God, particularly manifest in the idea of the present rule of Christ

---

38. Ibid., 229–31.
39. Ibid., 232.
40. Ibid.
41. Ibid., 241–42, 244.

("Christonomy"[42] or "Christocracy"[43]), is the biblical ground for the royal-priestly function of the church.[44] Yarnell rightly affirms that the direct kingship of Christ (i.e., his immediate presence in the church) guides the congregation to imitate his *triplex munus*—Christ as King, Priest, and Prophet who has made his people a "kingdom," a "priesthood," and a "prophethood" to govern communally, to worship corporately, and to proclaim convincingly.[45] While not distinct from Yarnell's theological assertion,[46] Garrett elsewhere explains the "lordship of Christ" first as a "declaration of his deity"—the "living Lord ... whose divine presence [is] with [his disciples] and in them is realized through the Holy Spirit"; and second, as an "indication of his dominion, or rulership" over the whole universe, primarily over the church.[47] Garrett, in this case, apparently correlates Christocracy (rule of Christ) with pneumatophoria (leadership of the Spirit). Garrett clarifies: "The Spirit's directive agency over and in the church is no contradiction to the headship of Jesus Christ over the church, for Christ's headship is administered by the Spirit."[48] Specifically, the Spirit realizes the lordship of Christ and leads the church of Christ by constant "rebuking, reforming, refining, renewing, and redirecting" so that the church may evade the snares of human "institutionalism" and hierarchical "ecclesiasticism" or religious sacerdotalism.[49] "Christocracy" and "pneumatophoria," though two distinct themes, bear the same basic meaning—the ultimate and immediate lordship of God in Christ through the Spirit directs and leads the life of the church.

Second, the divinely-given congregational authority to manage itself is not to be understood in a privatistic, individualistic, or narcissistic manner but in a corporate, communal, or congregational sense. Both Garrett

42. Yarnell, "Congregational Priesthood," 134.

43. Garrett notes, "Christ's kingship, which is both present and future and which has its prophetic and priestly aspects, means 'Christocracy'" (Garrett, *Systematic Theology*, 1:709).

44. Ibid., 2:644.

45. Yarnell, "Priesthood of Believers," 237.

46. See chapter 4, "The Ministry of the Church," for a detailed discussion on Garrett's understanding of the threefold pattern of Christ's royal (Isa 49:7; 52:12–15), prophetic (49:2; 50:4–5), and "priestly or sacrificial" (53:3–12) functions as the basic framework for the ministerial roles of the church (Garrett, *Systematic Theology*, 2:603, 607).

47. Ibid., 1:704–5.

48. Ibid., 2:209.

49. Ibid.

and Yarnell are persuaded that the royal priesthood in the New Testament does not primarily entail the notion of the direct, private, unhindered, or unmediated access to God's presence—which is properly a corollary of Christ's priesthood—simply because Christian-priests always need a mediated access to God through Christ who intercedes for them at the right hand of his Father.[50] First Peter 2:5–9; Revelation 1:5–6; 5:9–10; and 20:6 disclose the corporate nature and communal function of the priest-kings.[51] Yarnell states distinctly, "Because Christ is King and has made his people a kingdom [of priest-kings], they may rule themselves."[52] Both Yarnell and Garrett agree in principle that this divinely-given authority of communal governance within the royal priesthood denotes *neither* the idea of layman individualism—the layman having a right to oppose leadership freely by appealing to individual priesthood;[53] *nor* the practice of pastoral authoritarianism—the pastor having a right to dominate his congregation or, in Garrett's words, to "exclude church members from the decision-making of the congregation" by appealing to special priesthood.[54] The former may result in congregational "anarchism," the latter in pastoral "monarchism."[55] Rather, by virtue of the communal kingship of

---

50. Yarnell, "Priesthood of Believers," 240; Garrett, "Congregation-Led Church," 184.

51. Yarnell observes that the church is depicted in five "communal metaphors": "house," "priesthood," "nation," "race," and "people" (1 Pet 2:5, 9–10). Ontologically, "The inclusion of 'royal priesthood' within this list of ecclesial metaphors, along with the communal nature of the metaphor itself, argues strongly for a congregational understanding of the doctrine." Functionally, the royal priesthood is created to offer up "spiritual sacrifices," especially verbal proclamation of gospel; the church "functions in a mediatorial [or instrumental] manner in the proclamation of the gospel" (Yarnell, "Priesthood of Believers," 226, 227, 243). Garrett states that the central meaning of the royal priesthood is the "collective offering of spiritual sacrifices," which "places [communal] responsibility above [individual] privilege and servanthood above access" (Garrett, "Congregation-Led Church," 184).

52. Yarnell, "Priesthood of Believers," 237.

53. Ibid., 242. The doctrine of "private access" often insidiously transforms the priesthood doctrine into "the priesthood of every believer" and emphasizes the right, autonomy, and competence of individual soul before God apart from other Christian-priests. Subsequently, the "believer priest with his soul competency was elevated above the pastor and often pitted against the church" (237, 239).

54. Garrett, *Systematic Theology*, 2:633.

55. Garrett notes elsewhere, "When authority smothers freedom, authoritarianism will likely result, but when freedom reigns over authority, there will likely follow . . . individualism" that transforms the doctrine of the Christian priesthood to the doctrine of Christian papacy (Garrett, preface to the second edition of *Baptist Church Discipline*, vi).

the Christian priesthood and in view of the immediate lordship of Christ through his Spirit, the church, recognizing no inferior believer-priests and no superior governing bodies, consists of congregational priest-kings who serve the true King and Lord, Jesus Christ (Rev 19:16).

Third, the kingly or ruling function of the church is generally exercised in congregational polity and specifically expressed through church discipline. Garrett particularly uses three biblical passages pertaining to communal "discipline" (Matt 18:15–18; 1 Cor 5:2; 2 Cor 2:6) to argue for congregational polity.[56] Yarnell, on the other hand, uses 1 Corinthians 5–6 and Matthew 18:15–18, in conjunction with the "priest-kings" passages (Rev 1:4–8; 5:6–10; 20:4–6) to substantiate the concept of corporate kingship through church discipline.[57] Both Yarnell and Garrett concur that Matthew 18:15–18 and 1 Corinthians 5–6 provide biblical basis for communal authority in the matter of disciplining church members. Although nowhere in his priesthood doctrine does Garrett explain explicitly the church's "kingly" function, this does not mean that the "ruling" character of the Christian priesthood extends no influence to his ecclesiological reflection. In fact, his constant interest in congregational discipline precisely signifies the direct impact of the "ruling" function of the priesthood doctrine. Stated otherwise, although Garrett does not articulate a doctrine of Christian "priesthood-kingship" per se, his writings on congregational polity and/or authority with respect to church discipline demonstrate Garrett's creative and candid application of the governing or ruling authority of the priesthood.

Congregational Participation

As indicated by Garrett, while the New Testament expects Christians to obey and honor their civil government (Rom 13:1–7), Scripture does not speak distinctly on the issues of Christian participation in public office, military service, warfare, or revolution against the civil state.[58]

---

56. The other three passages Garrett uses for defending congregational polity deal with congregational decisions in choosing certain individuals for specific roles or tasks (Acts 6:3; 13:2–3; 15:22); see Garrett, "Congregation-Led Church," 159–70.

57. Yarnell, "Priesthood of Believers," 244.

58. Garrett, "Dialectic of Romans 13:1–7 and Revelation 13: Part Two," 20. It is noted that Garrett himself had planned to be enlisted for military service after college; however, because of his high myopia, he was denied of the opportunity and did not pursue such vocation any further (Garrett, "Baptist Identity and Christian Unity," 54).

Nonetheless, the church, in relation to the civil state, is definitely reminded to exercise and participate in the diakonal functions of "proclamation, witness, service, and self-giving love,"[59] the tasks that intimately connect to Garrett's understanding of the functions of the Christian priesthood.[60] As a case in point, Garrett, aspiring to maintain strict church-state separation, urges Christians, particularly Baptists, to participate corporately and responsibly in monetary support of their educational ministry, a form of participation which is reminiscent of the "stewardship" function of God's priestly people:[61]

> Let Baptists establish and retain only those institutions which they themselves can reasonably be expected to support and sustain. Let Baptists support these institutions generously and adequately. Let such institutions be unashamedly Christian and Baptist in their purpose. Let such institutions be of high quality without exception.[62]

Acknowledging the complexity of the issue of church-state relation/separation, Garrett, furthermore, emphatically calls for Christians, who are "in the world" but "not of the world" (John 17:11, 14, 16), to lead the transformation of the society in expression of the "responsibly prophetic role" of the church.[63] Christians and churches have endeavored "to change the society in which they have lived, whether to monogamous marriage, to the sacredness of human life, to the breakdown of class and caste, to the healing of bodily infirmities, to emancipation from slavery, or to political self-determination," remarks Garrett.[64] Although the questions as to whether Christians and churches should participate in civil office, military service, warfare, and revolution against totalitarian states remain

---

59. Garrett, "Biblical Basis of Religious Liberty," 285.

60. See "The Priesthood of Christians" in chapter 4, "The Ministry of the Church," for a review of the Christian priests' fourfold diakonal task—worship, witness, stewardship, and service.

61. Chapter 4, "The Ministry of the Church," has discussed Garrett's view on stewardship as one of the primary priestly functions. Garrett urges serious congregational participation through tithing-giving in supporting the "educational and diakonal ministries" and "evangelistic and missionary outreach" of the church (Garrett, *Systematic Theology*, 2:427).

62. Garrett, "Religious Liberty, Vatican Council II, and Baptists," 185.

63. Garrett, "Does Church-State Separation Necessarily Mean the Privatization of Religion?" 147.

64. Ibid.

untackled, Garrett is indubitably clear about Christians' participation in the priestly-prophetic function of the church to serve and transform the society.

In an attempt to answer the question, "Does church-state separation necessarily mean the privatization of religion?" Garrett incisively notes that church-state separation, wrongly interpreted, can lead to the notion of "individualistic and noncorporate" religion in which an individual Christian withdraws himself from participation in congregational life into his private or individualistic religiosity.[65] Garrett argues that "to be a Christian has been to be, in some sense, *in the church*"; religious freedom or "voluntaryism" signifies being "free and responsible in [one's] willingness to believe or not to believe and, having believed, to be free and responsible in one's expected decision to seek membership in some particular body of believers."[66] In short, a true believer ought to participate in the communal life of the body of believers. Christian faith, in this sense, does not represent a "privatization" of religion, but demands, conversely, participation in Christian fellowship. Christianity is expressed in the form of "a reconciled and reconciling fellowship" of people who have "come to Christ and to one another from various strata of society" (cf. Gal 3:28; Eph 2:13–18).[67] In and under Christ, no believer is superior or inferior to another believer in the Christian fellowship, regardless of cultural, racial, and economic backgrounds, and yet all believers equally participate in the body of Christ and the fellowship of Christians (Eph 2:19; 3:6).

Participation in the body of fellow Christians does not mean merely attending a certain church's events or programs but becoming members of a particular congregation and sharing in the congregational decision-making process. Through this congregational participation, Christian members are, in fact, sharing together in the process of spiritual maturity. Garrett reasons that by serving in differing ministries and by sharing in congregational meetings, all Christian members will "grow in faith and understanding and in love and fellowship" as they, in one accord, learn to seek the "mind and will of Christ." Consequently, the spiritual maturity of

---

65. Ibid., 145.
66. Ibid., 146; emphasis original.
67. Garrett, "Biblical Basis of Religious Liberty," 285.

the members will lead to a fuller participation in and identification with "the message, the ministry, and the mission of the congregation itself."[68]

For Garrett, the congregation-led polity—denoting members' participation and responsibility in all ecclesial decisions—is a logical corollary of his doctrine of royal priesthood. Garrett claims, "It is not difficult to perceive that there is an important connection between the priesthood of all Christians and congregation polity, especially when the latter is understood as the Congregational governance by all the believers."[69] Garrett asks forthrightly, "If all the believers are to exercise the 'royal priesthood' (1 Pet 2:9) through the offering of various spiritual sacrifices, then why should not those same believers together participate in and be responsible for the decision-making of the congregation?"[70] Garrett states, in effect, that *who they are* affects *what they do*. As royal priests, all Christian members are elected, enabled, and expected to participate together in directing, enriching, and shaping the mission, membership, ministry, and management of the congregation.

The entire Christian congregation is to be responsible for and participate in the church's life—from administration to ministration, from worship to witness, and from discipleship to discipline.[71] Garrett's emphasis on the active participation of the entire membership can be substantiated by two ecclesial aspects: pastoral ordination and church discipline.

First, Garrett perceives the congregation's common responsibility in the ordination of a pastor. Ordination is initiated, conducted, or even revoked by the entire Christian congregation. Garrett states:

> The examination of the ordinand normally focuses on conversion and call to ministry and on basic Christian doctrine, Christian ethics, and church practice. The laying on of hands is most often by all ordained pastors and deacons present but may include *the entire church membership*. Revocation of ordination, such as for theological or ethical reasons, is *by the congregation* of which the ordained person is a member.[72]

---

68. Garrett, "Congregation-Led Church," 186.
69. Ibid., 185.
70. Ibid.
71. Ibid., 157.
72. Garrett, *Systematic Theology*, 2:626; emphasis added.

Besides the practice that "members are both received into and excluded from a Baptist church by decision of the congregation,"[73] the obligation to examine, ordain, and, when necessary, to discipline a pastor also belongs to the whole church membership. This communal accountability does not by any means imply that the pastoral office or the ordained leadership is dispensable in the church's life. Garrett distinctly opposes the view that "congregational polity jeopardizes or cripples the legitimate roles of the ordained ministers . . . There is no either/or choice between such polity and such ordained ministry."[74] The roles of the lay members and the ordained ministers are not mutually exclusively.[75] Rather, the congregation should acknowledge the calling, the charisms, and the authority of its pastor to preach, care, and lead by his teaching and example. The congregation should also anticipate the servanthood of deacons, who share with their pastor in meeting the spiritual as well as physical needs of the congregation.[76] The leadership of the pastor and the servanthood of the deacons are coexistent and coextensive with congregation governance. The heart of the matter is that no leader or believer alone but the whole congregation is expected to participate in and decide on all the matters of the church, including the matter of ordination.

Second, the subject of church discipline discloses Garrett's constant emphasis on every member's full involvement in congregational life. He accents the responsibility of church discipline as belonging to "all church members," not merely in order to proclaim the gospel but also to "instruct, exhort, and admonish [fellow] Christians as to the well ordering of their lives in the fellowship of the body of Christ."[77] By the same token, Yoder, a Mennonite theologian, perceives the task of "binding and loosing" as belonging to the *ekklesia* (Matt 18:15–20), which denotes an "assembly, a gathering of a people into a meeting for deliberation or for

---

73. Garrett, "Congregation-Led Church," 189.

74. Ibid., 187. See also Garrett, "Under the Lordship," 125–27.

75. See chapter 4, "The Ministry of the Church," for a detailed discussion on the relation between the lay Christians and the ordained in church ministry.

76. Garrett, "Congregation-Led Church," 187–88. Garrett notes that the pastoral office bears an "authority of influence" rather than of domination and that deaconship is not to be conceived as membership on a "board of directors," which is a direct "violation of or deviation from Congregational polity. But, rightly interpreted in terms of its servant (*diakonos*) etymology and origin, the deaconship is a firm ally of Congregational polity" (188).

77. Garrett, "Church Discipline," 24.

a public announcement."[78] Every believer "in the Christian fellowship when aware of any kind of offense" that jeopardizes the fellowship of believers shares the responsibility to "take initiative toward the restoration of fellowship" (Matt 18:15).[79] The New Testament gives no inkling that the admonishing, forgiving, or reconciling responsibility lies only with a particular group of people, such as pastors, teachers, elders, bishops, preachers, or deacons, who are usually expected by the church to discipline the offender.[80] In the case that the offender remains impenitent, the church is to assume the congregational responsibility of "binding and loosing" instead of turning the person or issue over to civil authority or "to any other agency representing the total society," says Yoder.[81] Likewise, Garrett speaks unambiguously and forcefully about the congregational implementation of and participation in church discipline, arguing that "discipline initiated and administered *solely* by the minister would be a travesty of congregationalism"[82] or, more precisely, an outright denial of the priesthood of all believers.[83]

Congregational polity—participation and governance by the entire church membership in ecclesial matters—does not mean the church is always or automatically under the leadership of the Spirit (pneumatophoria). Garrett rightly warns: "Even the structures of congregational polity in the so-called 'free churches' can make the Spirit captive to culture or to the whims of a majority."[84] Especially in the process of congregational de-

---

78. Yoder, *Royal Priesthood*, 332. Yoder, preferring the phrase "binding and loosing," dislikes the term "discipline" because it often shifts the attention to the "punishment," the "offense," and the "standards," instead of the offender (343). Regardless of the term he chooses, Yoder holds to the basic premise that this ecclesial authority "to bind and to loose" does not belong to a few church officials but to all believing members (343–44).

79. Ibid., 329, 334.

80. Ibid., 334, 335.

81. Ibid., 335. Yoder observes that congregational authority "to bind and to loose" is founded on the confession of Jesus as Christ (Matt 16:16–19): "It is no accident that in Matthew 16 the assignment by Jesus of the power to bind and loose follows directly upon Peter's first confession of Christ as Messiah. The confession is the basis of authority; the authorization given is the seal upon the confession. The church is where, because there Jesus is confessed as Christ, men and women are empowered to speak to one another in God's name" (332).

82. Garrett, *Baptist Church Discipline*, 27; emphasis original.

83. Garrett, "Congregation-Led Church," 185, 188–89.

84. Garrett, *Systematic Theology*, 1:209. Garrett identifies three "twentieth-century examples of Protestant muzzling of the Holy Spirit," namely, "the defense of racial segre-

cisions, the guidance of the Spirit is indispensable. Yoder also points out that the Spirit has come not merely to "convince," "to lead into truth," and to remind the believers of Jesus' teachings (John 14:16, 26; 16:7–8) but also is "active especially in making decisions" in the church (Acts 13 and 15).[85] This "Spirit-led decision" process, nonetheless, is "orderly" in manner and "faithful" to the "biblical and theological heritage of Christian insight."[86] In a similar vein, writing on the Holy Spirit's leadership over the church, Garrett states:

> The lordship of the Holy Spirit is conveyed positively by his role as the guide to truth (John 16:3), as teacher of "all things" (John 14:26), and as sovereign in bestowing spiritual gifts (1 Cor 12:11) and negatively through the warnings against blasphemy against the Spirit (Mark 3:29 and par.), lying to the Spirit (Acts 5:3), grieving the Spirit (Eph. 4:30), and quenching the Spirit (1 Thess. 5:19).[87]

The leadership of the Spirit in the church, however, does not mean the reign of anarchism, subjectivism, or privatism. The "guidance by the Holy Spirit," while in harmony with the lordship of Christ, "must always be checked in the light of and by the norm of the canonical Scriptures."[88] Rather than keeping the Holy Spirit in bondage, the church ought to demonstrate "obedient response to the guidance of the Spirit."[89] By obediently seeking and understanding the mind of God under the lordship of Christ through the leadership of the Spirit as revealed and affirmed in Scripture, Christian members properly participate in the decision-making process, whether on the issues of ordination or discipline, to reach a divinely-authorized consensus.[90]

---

gation and discrimination, the acquiescence by some in political totalitarianism, and the surrender to suburban culture in the great cities" (ibid.).

85. Yoder, *Royal Priesthood*, 331.
86. Ibid., 342.
87. Garrett, *Systematic Theology*, 2:206–7.
88. Ibid., 2:209, 211.
89. Ibid., 2:209.
90. Ibid., 2:210–11; Garrett, "Under the Lordship," 129.

Communal Discipleship

The works of Garrett on religious liberty, congregational polity, and church discipline not only consistently exhibit the theme of congregational authority over and participation in all ecclesial matters but also essentially accentuate the practice of discipleship in the church.

First, Garrett repeatedly exhorts that congregational management is eventually aimed at discipleship. Congregational "polity is not an end but only a means to other ends—growth and maturity of Christians unto Christlikeness, the proclamation of the gospel to all nations and peoples, and the coming of the kingdom of God 'on earth as it is in heaven'" (Matt 6:10).[91] The congregation-led governance, as Garrett asserts, is more likely to cultivate and more capable of producing "loyal and responsible churchmanship," or "stronger, more mature Christians than other polities" because the Christian members are allowed and expected to participate in the process of decision-making on all matters of ministry and mission.[92] Every Christian member as a "minister" or a "missionary" becomes involved in fulfilling the mandate of discipleship (John 17:21; Matt 28:19; 1 Pet 2:9) by means of personal evangelism, short-term missions, or overseas evangelization.[93] The "gifted leaders," particularly pastors, are called to encourage and equip the entire congregation to assume the tasks of ministry or mission, which ultimately lead to the unity and maturity of the church (Eph 4:11–15).[94]

Garrett elsewhere theologizes that the "lordship of Christ," which is deemed as the primary foundation of congregational polity,[95] connotes "actual direction of the lives of his disciples through their obedient surrender to Jesus and increasing conformity to him."[96] The concept of Christ's lordship, signifying the presence of Christ through the Holy Spirit, directly mandates Christians and churches not merely to believe in Christ's deity and dominion but also to "*live out* the lordship of Jesus" through discipleship—"the imperative of obedience to his commands

---

91. Garrett, *Systematic Theology*, 2:645. Garrett emphatically quotes the statement again in "Congregation-Led Church," 194.

92. Garrett, "Congregation-Led Church," 193.

93. Ibid., 186–87.

94. Ibid., 186.

95. Ibid., 158.

96. Garrett, *Systematic Theology*, 1:704–6.

and conformity to his very nature."⁹⁷ Concisely, the lordship of Christ entails the obedient discipleship of all Christians, none excepted.⁹⁸ Thus, the congregational governance under the lordship of Christ, for Garrett, is ultimately intended for the purpose of mutual and communal discipleship, Christlikeness, and maturity of the whole body of Christ (Eph 4:11–15).⁹⁹

Second, congregational discipline is essentially correlated to discipleship.¹⁰⁰ Garrett frequently notes that the terms "discipline" and "discipleship" are based on the same Latin root word, *discere* (to learn).¹⁰¹ Church discipline is a useful means, in a negative sense, for "putting off the old man," deterring "moral decline" in the church, and preventing "eternal excommunication."¹⁰² Positively, church discipline can help "save the soul" of an individual and "safeguard the purity" of the congregation.¹⁰³ Commencing with rebuke or admonition (Matt 18:15–17) and concluding with disfellowshipping or excommunication (1 Cor 5) do not reflect a holistic view of church discipline. Its aim must ultimately be the redemption and restoration (i.e., discipleship) of the "offending brother." Furthermore, church discipline must be conducted in the spirit of repentance, forgiveness, and graciousness, without, at the same time, falling into "a neo-Pharisaic legalism" and compromising the purity and truthfulness of the church.¹⁰⁴

Despite the extent to which churches today are ignorant of or inimical to the concept and practice of church discipline, especially its "punitive"

---

97. Ibid., 1:705–6; emphasis added.

98. Garrett often connects the Great Commission (Jesus' command to "make disciples of all nations" in Matthew 28:19) with the function of the royal priesthood to proclaim Christ (1 Pet 2:9). In other words, the primary task of the priesthood is discipleship. See Garrett, "Congregation-Led Church," 186.

99. Ibid., 185–86; idem, *Systematic Theology*, 2:645. Estep incisively observes: "It is, of course, the concept that Christ is Lord and that of the corporate nature of all discipleship that keeps the concept of the priesthood of believers from degenerating into rank individualism." Estep, *Baptists and Christian Unity*, 171.

100. See the sections on "Born-again Membership" and "Disciplined Discipleship" in chapter 3, and "The Membership of the Church" for a review of the correlation between discipline and discipleship.

101. Garrett, "Church Discipline," 23; idem, *Baptist Church Discipline*, 5; idem, *Systematic Theology*, 2:380.

102. Garrett, "Church Discipline," 23; idem, *Baptist Church Discipline*, 12.

103. Garrett, "Congregation-Led Church," 168.

104. Garrett, *Baptist Church Discipline*, 27.

or "negative" dimension, Garrett indicates that to "neglect, abandon, or deny the validity of church discipline" is to deny "the authority of the New Testament" and thereby to deny the church's biblical mandate to discipleship.[105] On the one hand, church discipline must be initiated and exercised by the entire congregation, not by ordained ministers alone; on the other hand, its practice should focus on both "positive nurture and negative censures"—positive and negative discipline-discipleship—in anticipation of reducing the number of non-believing, uncommitted, or immature church membership while encouraging regenerate, dedicated, and disciplined churchmanship.[106]

Third, discipleship does not happen only within the church walls but also in the world, even in the midst of the tension of church-state separation. Garrett states: "Christians in particular are faced with the challenge of avoiding culture-religion on the one hand and exclusivist, other worldly withdrawal on the other. *Discipleship*, as never before, needs to be essential to membership" in order to cultivate a vital church.[107] Genuine and meaningful religious freedom does not call for people to become religious fanatics, pluralists, agnostics, atheists, or hermits, but instead calls for discipleship in churches to equip Christian members to advance vigorously the gospel of Christ in the society through the empowerment of the Spirit via biblical and legitimate means.[108] Garrett specifically admonishes that, instead of worldly weapons (2 Cor 10:4; Eph 6:11–12), the church and Christians have to rely constantly on "the gospel, the Bible, and the power, gifts, and leadership of the Holy Spirit" to "resist the nationalization, the politicization, and the acculturation of the Christian faith"[109] and, in the meantime, to "realize its [the church's] spiritual mission through its proclamation, its witness, its service, and its self-giving love,"[110] which are the spiritual functions of the Christian priesthood.

---

105. Garrett, "Church Discipline," 22.

106. Garrett, *Baptist Church Discipline*, 27; idem, "Seeking a Regenerate Church Membership," 34–36.

107. Garrett, "Religious Freedom: Why and How," 23; emphasis added.

108. Garrett observes that most "classical advocates of religious toleration and freedom believed in one God and the final accountability of all men to him. Today many advocate freedom of religion so as to be able to practice irreligion" (Garrett, "Religious Freedom: Why and How," 9–10).

109. Ibid., 16.

110. Garrett, "Biblical Basis of Religious Liberty," 285.

Christian priests, individually and corporately, are to become the *faithful followers of the Lord*, rather than the *freedom fighters of libertarianism*, in the continuous struggle for a proper church-state separation.

A church of Christ that is made up of true disciples of Christ is truly distinct and separate from the world or the civil state. Dulles perceives that the church that is a "community of disciples" is a "contrast society" as evidenced in the distinct and disciplined way of life of its members.[111] Furthermore, Dulles observes that "a new crisis for the Church arose after the conversion of Constantine, when Christianity became the established religion of the empire. Christians became increasingly involved in the ordinary tasks of civil life," including "government duties."[112] With the progressively obscured relation between the church and the state, the radical call to "renunciation" and "nonviolence" became increasingly irrelevant and even unreal to Christians.[113] Dulles, however, still perceives the perpetuation of the "ideal of discipleship," which is "a kind of interior discipleship, embracing the values and priorities upheld by Jesus."[114] Laypeople are not exempt from discipleship, specifically, "the responsibility to penetrate the secular sphere with the Spirit of Christ" via "introducing Christian norms into the worlds of business, government, and the professions," as well as marriage and parenthood.[115] Discipleship is not limited to a few vocational priests but is open to all Christian-priests.

In like manner, Garrett recognizes that the church's distinction and separation from the world does not necessarily mean that the church becomes "exclusivist" in the sense of its total withdrawal from the world, society, or culture.[116] Rather, as the "salt of the earth" and the "light of

---

111. Dulles, *Models of the Church*, 200. Dulles explains: In the New Testament, the "disciples," designation that is synonymous with "Christians" (Acts 6:2), maintained "a certain critical distance from its pagan environment. Frequently, it would appear, the faithful were required or at least strongly exhorted to abstain from engaging in war, from frequenting the baths and stadiums, and from wearing wigs and jewelry. Among themselves they practiced intense mutual love, caring for the poor and the sick, the widows and the orphans, and extending hospitality to travelers . . . Conscious of the demands of discipleship, the faithful were prepared for imprisonment, exile, and even death" (203).

112. Ibid., 204.

113. Ibid.

114. Ibid. Dulles speaks of discipleship as expressed in "self-abnegation, humble service, generosity toward the needy, and patience in adversity" (205).

115. Dulles, *Models of the Church*, 205.

116. Garrett, "Religious Freedom: Why and How," 23; idem, *Systematic Theology*, 2:704–5.

the world" (Matt 5:13–16), Christians and churches are called to make an impact on and bring transformation to the surrounding society.[117] Although Garrett does not specify whether or how Christians should take part in public office, military service, warfare, or revolution against the government, he, nonetheless, clearly adheres to a principle against using any civil weapons of violence, coercion, or legislation to fulfill the Great Commission of the church. A church is no longer a true community of Christ's disciples "when it adds or retains members by means of civil discrimination as well as by spurious tactics of evangelism . . . [or by] the coercive weapons of the civil state, whether its taxing power, or its legislative enactments, or its administrative power structures."[118] For Garrett, the church must and can only realize its identity and mission through the diakonal role of prophet-priests—"its proclamation, its witness, its service, [and] its self-giving love."[119]

CONCLUSION

Through a careful examination of Garrett's works on the "management" theme—church-state relations, congregational polity, and church discipline, this chapter comes to the conclusion that these writings are distinctly the application of Garrett's doctrine of the priesthood of all believers, especially with respect to the notions of corporate authority, congregational participation, and communal discipleship:

Authority—while showing the civil state its due respect, the entire local congregation as the people of God, body of Christ, and fellowship of the Spirit, and particularly, the "priest-kings" of God, must exercise corporate authority and spiritual responsibility over all matters of the church in obedience to the immediate lordship and leadership of God in Christ through the Spirit, without needing the intervention of any other external authority, political or otherwise.

---

117. Clowney argues, "There is every reason for the general office of the church 'laity' to consult together on political issues. So, too, the special officers of the church must provide biblical guidance and wisdom to assist in Christian analysis of political questions. The church has a prophetic role to perceive and expose ethical questions that underlie political issues. Where God has spoken in condemning sin, whether sodomy or financial exploitation, the church cannot be silent." Clowney, *Church*, 192–93.

118. Garrett, "Biblical Basis of Religious Liberty," 285.

119. Ibid. See also chapter 2, "The Mission of the Church" for a detailed discussion on church's functions in verbal proclamation and social services.

Participation—the entire Christian membership of a local church, not merely the specially called ministers, is expected to participate actively in the ministry and mission of the church, even in the matters of pastoral ordination and church discipline, and to function as God's priest-prophets to reach the unbelieving society via corporate and individual efforts in verbal evangelization and diakonal services.

Discipleship—the ultimate purpose of the exercise of an adequate separation of church and state, the practice of the divinely authorized congregational management, and the execution of communal discipline is to fulfill the distinctive calling of the priesthood of all believers, that is, to make genuine disciples of Christ within the church and in the world.

In summary, Garrett's approach to church-state relations, congregation-led polity, and communal discipline converges on the essential character of the royal priesthood; namely, the members of the entire congregation, rather than a few ordained pastors or deacons, are *equally responsible* for presiding over the life of the church, for participating in the mission and ministry of church, and for producing disciples within and beyond the church.

chapter 6

Garrett's Important Motifs in Perspective

AFTER EXPLORING AND EXAMINING Garrett's diverse writings under four major ecclesiological themes: mission, membership, ministry, and management, this chapter concludes that Garrett's doctrine of the priesthood of all believers is the essential motif that unifies the various ecclesiological issues and establishes his overall ecclesiology. To argue that the priesthood doctrine is the *sole* motif in Garrett's theology, however, is an overstatement because, first, Garrett himself does not distinctly see the doctrine as the only, though imperative, principle for a biblically balanced ecclesiology; and second, Garrett's ecclesiology reveals two other complementary, implicit but indispensable, underpinnings—the Trinity and discipleship in relation to the Christian priesthood.

THE INTEGRATIVE MOTIF: UNIVERSAL PRIESTHOOD

Chapter 2, "The Mission of the Church," demonstrates that Garrett's "mission" theme—"evangelization," "ecumenism," and "ethics"—consistently points to the universal, mediatory, and obligatory character of the Christian priesthood. The church's mission is universal because of God's initial intention to call and create a distinctly "peoplic" priesthood for the sake of reaching out to other nations (Exod 19:5–6). All Christians, instead of a select few, are enjoined and conjoined to fulfill the priestly obligation, functioning as a mediatory priesthood through evangelization by words and service to both Christians and non-Christians (1 Pet 2:9, 12). The result of the universal mission of the church is a universal priesthood made up of various peoples worthy of serving the living God (Rev 4:11; 5:8–9; 20:6).

With the priesthood motif, Garrett's topics on evangelization, ecumenism, and ethics are not multifaceted issues without coherence, but quite the contrary, they show unity in respect to people, posture, and purpose. In perspective, universal mission belongs to all Christians universally, both the ordained and the laity, as the divinely called, commissioned, and consecrated priesthood to fulfill the twofold function of verbal witness and diakonal action that may eventually bring about the salvation of non-Christians (i.e., human-God reconciliation) and the unity of Christians (i.e., human-human reconciliation), leading up to the ultimate consummation of the universal priesthood, the culmination that lies in the original intention of God.

Chapter 3, "The Membership of the Church," exhibits an intimate correlation between the "membership" theme—"believers' church concept," "believer's baptism by immersion," and "born-again membership"—and the priesthood motif, particularly pertaining to the aspects of regeneration-baptism, confession-commitment, and discipline-discipleship. Corresponding to the nature of the Christian priesthood, a believers' church belongs not to the few pastoral leaders or all people in general but to the regenerate–baptized members only. Admittedly, Scripture does not explicitly connect baptism to the priesthood passages; however, for Garrett, believer's baptism, which presupposes regeneration, is logically and theologically imperative to the admission to church membership and hence, the participation in the common priesthood.

Garrett's adamant insistence on "closed membership" is far from an unexpected aberration from his ecclesiology but reveals his profound integrity to the priesthood doctrine. As the priesthood is composed of believers by faith only, so also is the believers' church made up of members whose regenerate faith is evidenced in believer's baptism by immersion and in their continuous commitment to the life of the Christian community. In summary, Garrett's writings on the "membership" theme point to a theological correlation; namely, both the believers' church and the priesthood belong to the same group of people—the regenerated, baptized, committed Christians, rather than to a select few or the general public.

Chapter 4, 'The Ministry of the Church," affirms that Garrett's "ministry" theme is resolutely rooted in the essence of the priesthood doctrine—communal-mutual servanthood, universal-diversified unity, and equal-complementary ministry. The priestly-prophetic-princely ministry of Christ, though unique in and of itself, is in substance the pattern for the church's ministry, that is, the ministry of servanthood. This servant-ministry, which is essentially expressed in the forms of "spiritual sacrifices" of the royal priesthood—witness, worship, stewardship, and service, is open to all Christians. Both Christian members and ordained ministers, laity and leadership, are distinctly called and diversely gifted for the purpose of mutual service and complementary ministry that will eventually result in the maturity and unity of the church.

Despite the fact that Garrett does not reveal his position on the issue of women's ordination or pastorate, he nonetheless is clear with the intention not to divide the church, but to unite all Christian members, both men and women, as fellow priests for cooperative ministry. Being consistent with the priesthood notion that opens ministry to all Christians, Garrett is convinced that the ministry of the church should not be demarcated by gender, race, or socioeconomic background but defined by charisms, which are sovereignly, universally, and diversely bestowed by the Spirit. As God's fellow priests, all Christians are equal partners because all are indwelt, enabled, and gifted by the Spirit; and yet, not all are equally gifted in ministry, so that they may serve mutually and complementarily for the church's edification and God's glory.

Chapter 5, "The Management of the Church," reaches the conclusion that Garrett's writings on "church-state relations," "congregational polity," and "church discipline" are basically practical applications of his priesthood concept. Garrett applies the priesthood idea to congregational authority and accountability in all church matters—ministry-ministration, discipline-discipleship, orderliness-ordination, service-stewardship, and worship-witness—under the ultimate and immediate lordship of Christ through the leadership of the Spirit. While the Christian priesthood entails the active and full participation of all Christians in guiding, shaping, and impacting the entire fellowship, it denies neither the distinct authority of the pastor nor the separate role of the civil state.

Garrett's uncompromising stance on congregational governance does not grow out of his personal preference as a Baptist. Instead, the reason for the conviction lies in his faithful adherence to the communal, corporate, or congregational emphasis of the priesthood doctrine. Although everyone has a vote or voice in all church matters, no Christian member ought to act egoistically toward his fellow members or act intractably toward the church leadership. All members are supposed to be equipped and encouraged by the pastors or leaders of the church to fulfill the prophetic-priestly mission and ministry, whether within or beyond the church, without utilizing the worldly weapons of the state—violence, legislation, and coercion. Albeit there is no specific writing by Garrett expounding the "kingly" or "ruling" function of the priesthood, Garrett's accentuation on the final congregational authority over all spiritual matters, especially church discipline, without the intervention or interference of the state, is his direct application of his priesthood principle, which calls for the entire church, instead of the select few or the state, to manage itself responsibly and minister to others mutually.

In summary, Garrett's major themes of ecclesiology merge into a unitive perspective: all regenerate-baptized Christians—rather than the ordained leaders, the general public, or the civil government—are called, trusted, and expected to participate in universal witness, disciplined churchmanship, mutual ministry, and congregational governance, all of which unambiguously reflect the nature and function of the Christian priesthood, whether in the form of implication, correlation, derivation, or application.

THE INDISPENSABLE MOTIF: TRINITARIAN IMAGE

While the priesthood motif plays an integrative role in Garrett's overall ecclesiology, the Trinitarian theme becomes his underlying agenda. Except for "Authority for the Christian World Mission,"[1] Garrett does not structure other ecclesiological topics, at least not intentionally, around the Trinitarian concept. Nevertheless, to say that the concept is inconsequential to his ecclesiology would be a serious deficiency in discernment. In fact, the vestiges of the Trinitarian works have already been observed throughout the examined chapters.

In "The Mission of the Church," the Father creates, chooses, and calls forth a distinct priestly people through the propitiation, resurrection, and sending of the Son to fulfill the universal mission in the promise, presence, and power of the Holy Spirit. Without the call of the Father, the commission of Son, and the consecration of the Spirit, there is no Christian priesthood. The operational oneness of the triune God is the

---

1. Garrett, "Authority," 74–76.

indisputable ground for the unity of Christians and churches. Regardless of their distinctiveness and differences, Christians, individually and corporately, become participants of the universal priesthood called and commissioned to fulfill the mandate of the vertical (human-God) and horizontal (human-human) reconciliation.

The Trinitarian notion is inconspicuous but indispensable in "The Membership of the Church." In baptism by immersion, the person publicly identifies with the person of Christ in his death and resurrection and with the body of Christ in fellowship and discipleship. Only by faith in Christ and through the regeneration by the Spirit, as symbolically represented in believer's baptism, does the person enter into Christ's body and God's priesthood, both of which are concretely expressed in Garrett's concept of the believers' church. In other words, the believers' church, like Christ's body and God's priesthood, belongs only to those who confess Christ, who are born by the Spirit, and who commit to the priestly tasks of God.

The Trinitarian work is also integral in "The Ministry of the Church." While Christ's ministry of self-sacrificial service for the sake of sinners and saints is the principal pattern for the church, the power of the church to serve essentially lies in the Spirit. The Spirit's sovereign, universal, and diverse gifting of charisms to all Christians determines the church's direction and distribution of ministerial tasks. God may call certain individuals with the Spirit's charisms in preaching, teaching, and pastoring for special or ordained ministries as instituted and commissioned by Christ. Nonetheless, whether general-lay Christians or ordained-pastoral ministers, all should offer up "spiritual sacrifices" mutually and complementarily, in view of Christ's servanthood and the Spirit's charisms, for the ultimate glory of God in the maturity and unity of his church.

The Trinitarian presupposition is also vital in "The Management of the Church." The supremacy of God in the lordship of Christ through the leadership of the Spirit is the *raison d'être* that the church governs itself communally, that is, by the participation of all Christian members in decisions over all ecclesial matters without other external or superior interference. The Trinity's sovereign and present works define the identity and determine the role of the people of God. Stated another way, the result of the harmonic operation of the triune God is the Trinitarian identity of the church and the threefold function of the Christian priesthood: as the people of God, the body of Christ, and the fellowship of the Spirit, the church should and must fulfill the kingly-prophetic-priestly function—to govern the church corporately, to proclaim the Word persuasively, and to serve the people sacrificially.

In summary, all of Garrett's major themes exhibit the Trinitarian role in the life of the church. Who God is and what the Trinity did, does, and will do shape the identity, conduct, role, or function of the church, from its inception until the *eschaton*. The primary corollary of the triune God and his works is the Trinitarian image of the church—the people of God, the body of Christ, and the fellowship of the Spirit. A logical corollary of the church's Trinitarian identity is the priesthood of all Christians. The triune God is ultimately engaged in the purpose, process, and perfection of the peoplic priesthood.

THE INTRINSIC MOTIF: DISCIPLINED DISCIPLESHIP

Besides the Trinitarian image, Garrett's ecclesiology also evinces the idea of discipleship inherently connected to the priesthood doctrine.

All Christians, ordained pastors or laypeople, as participants of the universal priesthood must fulfill the universal mission as the agents of the gospel by preaching and reaching out to all nations at all times in all places by all means. While the salvific, sanctifying, and consummating work lies ultimately in the Trinity, the royal priesthood carries the responsibility of not merely producing confessed believers but also making committed disciples who are willing to fulfill the commission of human-God and human-human reconciliation, by means of global evangelism to unbelievers, critical-conversional-constructive conversations among Christian churches, and diakonal services to all people, Christian or non-Christian.

Garrett's firm teaching on the interrelated concepts of the believers' church, regenerate membership, closed membership, and believer's baptism is his aspiration and appeal for the disciplined discipleship of God's people. Baptism by immersion is not simply an external enactment of the internal regeneration of the baptized by the Spirit, but also an entailment of one's commitment to the disciplined life in the community of faith. Consequently, the practice of infant or child baptism without requiring conscious, confessed, and committed faith undoubtedly severs the link between the call for baptism and the practice of discipleship. Admitting the regenerate, baptized, confessed, and committed members, on the other hand, ensures the faithful fulfillment of the church's priestly function of the Great Commission, whether in the form of global evangelism, mutual edification, or communal discipleship.

To emulate the mission and ministry laid down by Christ, churches and Christians are equally missionaries and ministers to others in order to procure and produce disciples. The ordained pastors or ministers, who receive special callings, charisms, and commitments to preach, teach, and lead, must fulfill the responsibility of equipping believers for the priestly function, that is, active witness through words or deeds. Based on the universal and diverse gifts from the Spirit, both laity and leadership are obliged to mutual and complementary servanthood. Garrett's plea for the entire participation of the Christian members, including women, in the primary priestly function—worship, witness, stewardship, and service—is eventually for the unity, edification, maturity, or Christlikeness of the body of Christ, which is the essence of discipleship.

Finally, the topics of church-and-state relations, congregational polity, and church discipline reveal Garrett's consistent concern for discipleship. The call for strict separation of church and state is not to encourage passivity or disengagement but to persuade the church to make true disciples in the world by relying faithfully on the Bible, the gospel, and the Spirit, without utilizing the violent, coercive, or judicial weapons of the world. Rather than being under the authority of the civil state, the church must manage itself corporately under the immediate lordship of Christ and the present guidance of the Spirit. This form of congregational management is the most efficient way of producing discipleship, as the entire Christian membership is involved in seeking God's direction and instruction in one accord on all ecclesial matters. Even in the matter of church discipline, its ultimate goal does not stop at exhortation or excommunication but discipleship—cultivating committed, disciplined, and mature members to realize the spiritual mission of the church through gospel proclamation and diakonal ministry.

In conclusion, the present writer has demonstrated that, while the Trinitarian and discipleship doctrines play an indispensable and intrinsic role, the concept of the believers' priesthood is primarily a unifying motif of Garrett's overall ecclesiology.

SUGGESTIONS FOR POTENTIAL AND FURTHER RESEARCH

Despite the interactions with the theologians from various Christian denominations throughout the chapters, there is still much room for further investigation and dialogues pertaining to Garrett's interpretation and implication of the priesthood doctrine: (1) One may compare and contrast Garrett's ecclesiology with that of the Pentecostal-Charismatic theologians, especially with respect to the crucial role of the Holy Spirit in the doctrine of the Christian priesthood. (2) Further research may also focus on the topic of lay preachers or lay theologians by placing Garrett's priesthood doctrine alongside Wesleyan-Methodist ecclesiology. (3) The issue of pastoral and congregational authority may shed further light by setting Garrett's priesthood notion against those of the Anglican and Lutheran traditions, particularly in view of the lordship of Christ.

TOWARD A BALANCED, BIBLICAL, BAPTIST THEOLOGY

Garrett's ecclesial methodology that is explicitly centralized in the doctrine of the Christian priesthood, implicitly connected to the doctrine of the Trinity, and inherently coalesced into the doctrine of discipleship, indicates a solid way of constructing a balanced, biblical, and Baptist ecclesiology:

Balanced: The priesthood doctrine without the Trinitarian notion may lead to a privatistic, atomistic, or anthropocentric ecclesiology. The priesthood doctrine without the discipleship notion may eventually become a theoretical ecclesiology. Positively, the doctrine that is intentionally founded on all three notions will forge an ecclesiology that is doctrinally solid and pastorally valid. Thus, Garrett's threefold principle may function to balance orthodoxy and orthopraxy.

Biblical: The priesthood, Trinitarian, and discipleship themes are essentially derived from Scripture itself. No Christian church or evangelical denomination denies any of the three basic beliefs, despite the fact that one may overemphasize or deemphasize one or the other. By carefully and deliberately utilizing all these concepts, a theologian may build a biblically grounded ecclesiology that will establish common grounds with other Christian heritages and, subsequently, bridge the theological gap between Baptists and other Christian traditions.

Baptist: By faithful interpretation of and adherence to the priesthood doctrine, Garrett's aim is not a compromise of truths but a formation of

Baptist identity and distinctives. The biblically balanced explication of the universal priesthood in connection with the Trinitarian and discipleship idea necessarily involves and implies the convictions of corporate evangelistic obligation in proclamation and service, closed membership with believer's baptism by immersion, complementary ministry of the laity and leadership, and congregation-led discipline-discipleship within and beyond the church. Without any of the four elements, there would not be a proper Baptist ecclesiology.

CONCLUSION

The doctrine of the church has supposedly caused disunity, disorientation, and disorderliness within the church. Nonetheless, Garrett's ecclesiology, essentially rooted in the doctrine of the priesthood of all believers and supported by the Trinitarian and discipleship conception, has pointed the way to and laid the foundation for an ecclesiology that aims at restoring church unity, reconnecting doctrine-practice, and rediscovering Baptist identity. Such an ecclesiology deserves the attention of all churches, Baptists or otherwise.

Bibliography

PRIMARY SOURCES

Garrett, James Leo, Jr. "A Christian View of Material Things." In *Resource Unlimited: Christian Stewardship—From Theology to Ecology from Motives to Methods*, edited by William L. Hendricks, 83–96. Nashville: Stewardship Commission of the Southern Baptist Convention, 1972.

———. *Advocates of Religious Toleration and Freedom*. Waco, TX: Baylor University Book Store, 1978.

———. "Analysis: Should Baptist Churches Adopt Open Membership? No," *Baptist Standard*, April 26, 2010, 10.

———. "Are Southern Baptists 'Evangelicals'? A Further Reflection." In *Southern Baptists and American Evangelicals: The Conversation Continues*, edited by David S. Dockery, 218–23. Nashville: Broadman & Holman, 1993.

———. "Authority for the Christian World Mission." In *Christ for the World*, edited by G. Allen West Jr., 73–82. Nashville: Broadman, 1963.

———. *Baptist Church Discipline: A Historical Introduction to the Practices of Baptist Churches, with Particular Attention to the Summary of Church Discipline Adopted in 1773 by the Charleston Association*. Nashville: Broadman, 1962; rev. ed., Paris, AR: Baptist Standard Bearer, 2004.

———. "Baptist Distinctives: Endangered Species" (chapel message). Fort Worth: Southwestern Baptist Seminary, September 4, 1991. Photocopy.

———. "Baptist Identity and Christian Unity: Reflections on a Theological Pilgrimage." *American Baptist Quarterly* 24 (2005): 53–66.

———, ed. *Baptist Relations with Other Christians*. Valley Forge, PA: Judson, 1974.

———. *Baptist Theology: A Four-Century Study*. Macon, GA: Mercer University Press, 2009.

———. *Baptists and Roman Catholicism: A Survey of Baptist Writings about the Roman Catholic Church, with an Interpretation of Recent Developments*. Nashville: Broadman, 1965.

———. *Baptists and the Awakenings of Modern History*. Fort Worth, TX: n.p., 1959.

———. "Baptists concerning Baptism: Review and Preview." *Southwestern Journal of Theology* 43 (2001): 52–67.

———. "Basic Theological Differences." In *Revolt and Commitment: A Summary Report of Discussions at a Protestant Council on Roman Catholicism Convened at Buck Hill*

Falls, Pennsylvania, April 19–21, 1960, edited by Stuart P. Garver, 28–30. Sea Cliff, NY: Christ's Mission, 1960.

———. "Biblical Authority according to Baptist Confessions of Faith." *Review and Expositor* 76 (1979): 43–54.

———. "Biblical Infallibility and Inerrancy according to Baptist Confessions." *Search* 3 (1972): 42–45.

———. "Bureaucratic Governmental Regulation of Churches and Church Institutions." *Journal of Church and State* 21 (1979): 195–207.

———, ed. *Calvin and the Reformed Tradition*. Christian Classics. Nashville: Broadman, 1980.

———. "Chapel: April 11, 1997." Fort Worth: Southwestern Baptist Seminary, 1997. Audiocassette.

———. "Church Discipline: Lost but Recoverable." *Founders Journal* 4 (1991): 21–24.

———. "Civil Religion: Clarifying the Semantic Problem." *Journal of Church and State* 16 (1974): 187–95.

———. "Doctrinal Authority, 1925–1975: A Study in Four Representative Baptist Journals." *Foundations* 22 (1979): 3–12.

———. "Does Church-State Separation Necessarily Mean the Privatization of Religion?" In *Readings on Church and State*, edited by James E. Wood Jr., 141–48. Waco, TX: J. M. Dawson Institute of Church-State Studies, 1989.

———. "Ecclesiology: The Crucial Issue." *Baptist Standard*, October 14, 1954, 6–7; October 21, 1954, 8.

———. "Evangelism and Social Involvement." *Southwestern Journal of Theology* 12 (1970): 51–62.

———. *Evangelism for Discipleship*. Louisville, KY: n.p., 1964.

———. "Free Exercise Clause of the First Amendment: Retrospect and Prospect." *Journal of Church and State* 17 (1975): 393–98.

———. "Garrett: 'Should Southern Baptists Adopt the Synod of Dort?'" *Baptists Today*, June 26, 1997, 18–19.

———, ed. "Grace: Roman Catholic-Southern Baptist Dialogue (1982–1984)." *Southwestern Journal of Theology* 28 (1986): 4–119.

———. "Historical Theology: 1945–1965." *Southwestern Journal of Theology* 7 (1965): 77–82.

———. "History of Christian Doctrine: Retrospect and Prospect." *Review & Expositor* 68 (1971): 245–60.

———. "John A. Mackay on the Roman Catholic Church." *Journal of Presbyterian History* 50 (1972): 111–28.

———. "Luther's Developing Doctrine of Baptism." In *The Teacher's Yoke: Studies in Memory of Henry Trantham*, edited by E. Jerry Vardaman and James Leo Garrett Jr., 203–14. Waco, TX: Baylor University Press, 1964.

———. "Major Emphases in Baptist Theology." *Southwestern Journal of Theology* 37 (1995): 36–46.

———. "Missions and Baptist Systematic Theologies." *Baptist History and Heritage* 35 (2000): 67–71.

———. "Outside the Church No Salvation." *Baptist Standard*, September 10, 1958, 6–7.

———. "Polemic, Conversion, and/or Dialogue: Baptist Postures toward the Roman Catholic Church." *Review & Expositor* 60 (1963): 319–42.

———. "Prayer." In *Encyclopedia of Southern Baptists*, 2:1102–3. Nashville: Broadman, 1971.

———. "Problems, Issues, and Challenges in Christian Unity." In *New People for a New World: Official Report of the Thirteenth Congress, Baptist World Alliance, Stockholm, Sweden, July 8–13, 1975*, edited by Cyril E. Bryant and Debbie Stewart, 201–07. Nashville: Broadman, 1975.

———. "Professor Examines Historical Role of Deacons." *Baptist and Reflector*, August 14, 1991, 4; August 21, 1991, 4.

———. "Protestant Writings on Roman Catholicism in the United States between Vatican Council I and Vatican Council II: An Analysis and Critique in View of the Contemporary Protestant Roman Catholic Confrontation." PhD diss., Harvard University, 1966.

———. "Protestant-Catholic Dialogue: A Baptist View." *Christianity Today*, October 23, 1964, 13–15.

———. "Reappraisal of Chalcedon." *Review & Expositor* 71 (1974): 31–42.

———. "Recovering My Priesthood." *Home Missions*, February 1965, 14–15.

———. *Reinhold Niebuhr on Roman Catholicism*. Louisville, KY: Seminary Baptist Book Store, 1972.

———. "Religious Freedom: Church and State." *The Canadian Baptist* 129 (1983): 6–10.

———. "Religious Freedom: Why and How in Today's World." *Southwestern Journal of Theology* 18 (1976): 9–24.

———. "Religious Liberty, Vatican Council II, and Baptists." *Review and Expositor* 62 (1965): 175–85.

———. "Representative Modern Baptist Understandings of Biblical Inspiration." *Review and Expositor* 71 (1974): 179–95.

———. "Restitution and Dissent among Early English Baptists, Part 1." *Baptist History and Heritage* 12 (1977): 193–210, 251.

———. "Restitution and Dissent among Early English Baptists: Representative Late Sixteenth and Early Seventeenth Century Sources, Part 2." *Baptist History and Heritage* 13 (1978):11–27.

———. "Roman Catholicism and Baptist Missions." Paper delivered at the Conference for Furloughing Missionaries in Detroit, MI, May 21, 1966.

———. "Seeking a Regenerate Church Membership." *Southwestern Journal of Theology* 3 (1961): 25–36.

———. "Sources of Authority in Baptist Thought." *Baptist History and Heritage* 13 (1978): 41–49.

———. "Southern Baptists as Evangelicals." *Baptist History and Heritage* 18 (1983): 10–20.

———. "Southern Baptists, Evangelicals, and Southwestern." *Southwestern News*, Fall 2002, 6–9.

———. "Studies of the Sixteenth Century Protestant Reformation: The Literature in English 1946–1966." *Review & Expositor* 64 (1967): 207–25.

———. *Systematic Theology: Biblical, Historical, and Evangelical*. 2 vols. 2nd ed. North Richland Hills, TX: BIBAL, 2000, 2001.

———. *Systematic Theology: Biblical, Historical, and Evangelical*. 2 vols. 2nd ed. In Ages Digital Library [CD-ROM]. Albany, OR: Ages Software, 2006.

———. *Systematic Theology: Biblical, Historical, and Evangelical*. Vol. 1. 3rd ed. North Richland Hills, TX: Bibal, 2007.

———. "The Authority of the Bible for Baptists." *Southwestern Journal of Theology* 41 (1999): 4–40.

———. "The Bible at Southwestern Seminary during Its Formative Years: A Study of H. E. Dana and W. T. Conner." *Baptist History and Heritage* 21 (1986): 29–43.

———. "The Biblical Basis of Religious Liberty." In *The Truth that Makes Men Free: Official Report of the Eleventh Congress, Baptist World Alliance, Miami Beach, Florida, U.S.A., June 25-30, 1965*, edited by Josef Nordenhaug. Nashville: Broadman, 1966.

———. "The Biblical Doctrine of the Priesthood of the People of God." In *New Testament Studies: Essays in Honor of Ray Summers in His Sixty-Fifth Year*, edited by Huber L. Drumwright Jr. and Curtis Vaughan, 137–49. Waco, TX: Baylor University Press, 1975.

———. "The Christian Doctrine of Reconciliation." Paper delivered to the Texas Baptist Pastors' Reconciliation Forum, North Texas Conference Center at Camp Copass, Denton, TX, February 5, 1999.

———, ed. *The Concept of the Believers' Church: Addresses from the 1967 Louisville Conference*. Scottdale, PA: Herald, 1970.

———. "The Congregation-Led Church: Congregational Polity." In *Perspectives on Church Government: Five Views of Church Polity*, edited by Chad Owen Brand and R. Stanton Norman, 157–208. Nashville: Broadman & Holman, 2004.

———. "The Dialectic of Romans 13:1–7 and Revelation 13: Part One." *Journal of Church and State* 18 (1976): 433–42.

———. "The Dialectic of Romans 13:1–7 and Revelation 13: Part Two." *Journal of Church and State* 19 (1977): 5–20.

———. "The Distinctive Identity of Southern Baptists vis-à-vis Other Baptists." *Baptist History and Heritage* 31 (1996): 6–16.

———. "The Kingdom of God according to Baptist Theology." *Southwestern Journal of Theology* 40 (1998): 53–68.

———. "The Nature of the Church according to the Radical Continental Reformation." *Mennonite Quarterly Review* 32 (1958): 111–27.

———. "The Pre-Cyprianic Doctrine of the Priesthood of all Christians." In *Continuity and Discontinuity in Church History: Essays Presented to George Huntston Williams on the Occasion of His 65th Birthday*, edited by F. Forrester Church and Timothy George, 45–61. Leiden: E. J. Brill, 1979.

———. "The Priesthood of All Believers." *Capital Baptist*, October 24, 1962, 4.

———, ed. "The Priesthood of All Christians." *Southwestern Journal of Theology* 30 (1988): 3–54.

———. "The Priesthood of All Christians: From Cyprian to John Chrysostom." *Southwestern Journal of Theology* 30 (1988): 22–33.

———. "The Shifting Foci of the Protestant-Roman Catholic Confrontation: Peter, Mary, and the Sacraments." *Review and Expositor* 68 (1971): 29–41.

———. "The Teaching of Recent Southern Baptist Theologians on the Bible." In *The Proceedings of the Conference on Biblical Inerrancy 1987*. Nashville: Broadman, 1987.

———. "The Theology and Practice of Baptism: A Southern Baptist View." *Southwestern Journal of Theology* 28 (1986): 65–72.

———. "The Theology of Walter Thomas Conner." ThD. diss., Southwestern Baptist Theological Seminary, 1954.

———. "Theology of Prayer." *Southwestern Journal of Theology* 14 (1972): 3–17.

———. "Thomas Aquinas' Doctrine of Penance: A Critical Analysis." ThM thesis, Princeton Theological Seminary, 1949.
———. "Under the Lordship of Christ through Democratic Processes." In *Upon This Rock: The Baptist Understanding of the Church*, edited by Jason G. Duesing, Thomas White, and Malcolm B. Yarnell. Nashville: B&H, 2010.
———. "Understanding the Church: A Southern Baptist Perspective." *The Theological Educator* 39 (1989): 60–66.
———. "Vital Issues for Southern Baptists." *Southwestern News*, May 1952, 2.
———. "Vital Issues for Southern Baptists: 1968." *Quarterly Review* 28 (1968): 24–27.
———, ed. *We Baptists*. Franklin, TN: Providence House, 1999.
———. "Who Are Southern Baptists in 1989?" *Baptist Standard*, July 26, 1989, 12.
———. "Why Systematic Theology?" *Criswell Theological Review* 3 (1989): 259–81.
Garrett, James Leo Jr., et al. *Are Southern Baptists 'Evangelicals'?* Macon, GA: Mercer University Press, 1983.
Garrett, James Leo, et al. "Dr. James Leo Garrett." Fort Worth, TX: Southwestern Baptist Theological Seminary, 2008. Compact disc.

SECONDARY SOURCES

Althouse, Peter. "Towards a Pentecostal Ecclesiology: Participation in the Missional Life of the Triune God." *Journal of Pentecostal Theology* 18 (2009): 230–45.
Avis, Paul D. L. "Luther's Theology of the Church." *Churchman* 97 (1983): 104–11.
———, ed. *The Christian Church: An Introduction to the Major Traditions*. London: SPCK, 2002.
Ayres, Francis O. *The Ministry of the Laity: A Biblical Exposition*. Philadelphia: Westminster, 1962.
Bailey, Raymond. "Multiple Ministries and Ordination." *Review & Expositor* 78 (1981): 531–37.
Balthasar, Hans Urs von. "Wer ist ein Laie." *Internationale Katholische Zeitschrift Communio* 14 (1985): 385–91.
Barth, Karl. *The Teaching of the Church regarding Baptism*. Translated by Ernest A. Payne. London: SCM, 1948; reprint, Eugene, OR: Wipf & Stock, 2006.
Basden, Paul A. "James Leo Garrett, Jr." In *The Legacy of Southwestern: Writings that Shaped a Tradition*, edited by James Leo Garrett Jr., 132–47. North Richland Hills, TX: Smithfield, 2002.
———. "James Leo Garrett Jr." In *Theologians of the Baptist Tradition*, edited by Timothy George and David Dockery, 297–316. Nashville: Broadman & Holman, 2001.
Basden, Paul A., and David S. Dockery, eds. *The People of God: Essays on the Believers' Church*. Nashville: Broadman & Holman, 1991.
Beasley-Murray, George R. *Baptism in the New Testament*. Grand Rapids: Eerdmans, 1962.
———. "The Authority and Justification for Believers' Baptism." *Review & Expositor* 77 (1980): 63–70.
Beckwith, Roger T. "The Relation between Christ's Sacrifice and Priesthood and Those of the Church: An Attempt at a Summary Statement." *Churchman* 103 (1989): 231–39.
Belonick, Deborah. "The Spirit of the Female Priesthood." In *Women and the Priesthood*, edited by Thomas Hopko, 135–68. Crestwood, NY: St Vladimir's Seminary, 1983.
Bennett, G. Willis. "The Authority of the Undershepherd and the Power of the Congregation." *Ogbomoso Journal of Theology* 4 (1989): 25–29.

Bergendoff, Conrad John Immanuel, ed. "Wanted: A Theory of the Laity in the Lutheran Church." *Lutheran Quarterly* 3 (1951): 82–90.
Berkouwer, Gerrit C. *The Church*. Grand Rapids: Eerdmans, 1976.
Besch, Günter. "Amt und Allgemeines Priestertum in den Kirchen der Diaspora." In *Vom Amt des Laien in Kirche und Theologie: Festschrift für Gerhard Krause zum 70. Geburtstag*, edited by Henning Schröer and Gerhard Müller, 299–310. New York: Walter De Gruyter, 1982.
Best, Ernest. "1 Peter 2:4–10: A Reconsideration." *Novum Testamentum* 11 (1969): 270–93.
———. *One Body in Christ*. London: SPCK, 1955.
———. "Spiritual Sacrifice: General Priesthood in the New Testament." *Interpretation* 14 (1960): 273–99.
Bianchi, Eugene C., and Rosemary Radford Ruether, eds. *A Democratic Catholic Church: The Reconstruction of Roman Catholicism*. New York: Crossroad, 1992
Block, Kenneth B. "The People of God, the Communion of Saints, and the Priesthood of All Believers." In *Martin Luther, Companion to the Contemporary Christian*, edited by Robert Kolb and David Lumpp, 37–48. St. Louis, MO: Concordia, 1982.
Bloesch, Donald. *The Church: Sacraments, Worship, Ministry, Mission*. Downers Grove, IL: InterVarsity, 2002.
Boff, Leonardo. "Ecclesiogenesis: Ecclesial Basic Communities Re-Invent the Church." *Mid-Stream* 20 (1981): 431–88.
Bonhoeffer, Dietrich. *The Cost of Discipleship*. Translated by R. H. Fuller. New York: Touchstone, 1995.
Braaten, Carl E. *Mother Church: Ecclesiology and Ecumenism*. Minneapolis: Fortress, 1998.
Brackney, William H. "Landmarkism." In *Historical Dictionary of the Baptists*. 2nd ed., 331–33. Lanham, MD: Scarecrow, 2009,.
Bradshaw, Paul F. "Patterns of Ministry." *Studia Liturgica* 15 (1983): 49–64.
Brand, Chad O. Review of *Systematic Theology: Biblical, Historical, and Evangelical*, vol. 2, by James Leo Garrett. *Journal of the Evangelical Theological Society* 42 (1999): 522–24.
Brand, Chad O., and R. Stanton Norman, eds. *Perspectives on Church Government: Five Views of Church Polity*. Nashville: Broadman & Holman, 2004.
Brandner, Tobias. "Authority in the Church: Some Reformation Based Reflections about the Ministry in the Church, also with Regard to the Churches in China." *Asia Journal of Theology* 21 (2007): 135–46.
Breward, Ian. "Ministerial and/or Royal Priesthood." *Reformed Theological Review* 29 (1970): 1–11.
Bromiley, Geoffrey W. "Baptismal Regeneration." In *Evangelical Dictionary of Theology*, edited by Walter A. Elwell. 2nd ed., 135. Grand Rapids: Baker, 2001.
Brunner, Peter. "Sacerdotium und Ministerium: Ein Diskussionsbeitrag in 9 Thesen." *Kerygma und Dogma* 18 (1972): 101–17.
Calvin, John. *Institutes of Christians Religion*. Translated by Ford Lewis Battles. 4 vols. In *John Calvin Collection* [CD-ROM]. Albany, OR: Ages Software, 1998.
Carvin, Walter P. "Sacrifice and Priesthood in the Evangelical Tradition." *Foundations* 2 (1959): 332–39.
Chapple, Richard Curtis Jr. "Rediscovering Salvation as a Requirement for Full Membership." *AME Zion Quarterly Review* 109 (1997): 26–35.
Chempakassery, Philip. "Ecumenism and the Trinitarian Ecclesiology." *Christian Orient* 24 (2003): 178–84.

Cheung, Alex T. M. "The Priest as the Redeemed Man: A Biblical-Theological Study of the Priesthood." *Journal of the Evangelical Theological Society* 29 (1986): 265–75.
Child, Robert L. "Priesthood of All Believers." *Baptist Quarterly* 16 (1955): 99–108.
Chin, Soh Guan. *A Trinitarian Covenantal Theology of the Church*. Lincoln, NE: iUniversity Press, 2000.
Chryssavgis, John. "The Royal Priesthood (Peter 2:9) [sic]." *Greek Orthodox Theological Review* 32 (1987): 373–77.
Clark, Robert. "The Imperial Priesthood of the Believer (Revelation 1:6; 1 Peter 2:5, 9)." *Bibliotheca Sacra* 92 (1935): 442–49.
Clowney, Edmund. *The Biblical Doctrine of the Church*. Philadelphia: Westminster, 1979.
———. *The Church*. Downers Grove, IL: InterVarsity, 1995.
Coffey, David. "The Common and the Ordained Priesthood." *Theological Studies* 58 (1997): 209–36.
Coleran, James E. "The Sacrifice of Melchisedech." *Theological Studies* 1 (1940): 27–36.
Congar, Yves. *Lay People in the Church: A Study for a Theology of Laity*. Translated by Donald Attwater. Westminster, MD: Newman, 1965.
Cowan, Steven B., ed. *Who Runs the Church? Four Views on Church Government*. Grand Rapids: Zondervan, 2004.
Crawford, John Richard. "Calvin and the Priesthood of All Believers." *Scottish Journal of Theology* 21 (1968): 145–56.
Criswell, Wallie A. *The Doctrine of the Church*. Nashville: Convention, 1980.
Cross, F. L., and Elizabeth A. Livingstone, eds. "Baptism." In *Dictionary of the Christian Church*. 3rd ed., 150–52. Peabody, MA: Hendrickson, 2007.
Dagg, John L. *A Treatise on Church Order*. Paris, AR: Baptist Standard Bearer, 2006.
Daley, Brian E. "The Ministry of Disciples: Historical Reflections on the Role of Religious Priests." *Theological Studies* 48 (1987): 605–29.
Dana, Harvey E. *A Manual of Ecclesiology*. 2nd ed., revised in collaboration with L. M. Sipes. Kansas City, KS: Central Seminary Press, 1944.
Dargan, Edwin C. *Ecclesiology: A Study of the Churches*. Louisville, KY: Charles T. Dearing, 1905.
Davidson, Minor. "Southern Baptists and the Doctrine of the Priesthood of All Believers." ThD diss., Southwestern Baptist Theological Seminary, 1966.
Davis, H. Francis. "The Priesthood of the Faithful." *Downside Review* 69 (1951): 155–70.
DeSilva, David Arthur. "The Invention and Argumentative Function of Priestly Discourse in the Epistle to the Hebrews." *Bulletin for Biblical Research* 16 (2006): 295–323.
Dever, Mark. *Nine Marks of a Healthy Church*. Wheaton, IL: Crossway, 2004.
———. "The Priesthood of All Believers." In *The Compromised Church: The Present Evangelical Crisis*, edited by John H. Armstrong, 85–116. Wheaton, IL: Crossway, 1998.
Deweese, Charles W. *Women Deacons and Deaconesses: 400 Years of Baptist Service*. Macon, GA: Mercer University Press, 2005.
Dieter, Theodor. "Ordained Ministry and Priesthood of All the Baptized according to the Lutheran Tradition." *Theology & Life* 29 (2006): 171–86.
Dillon, Richard J. "Biblical Approaches to the Priesthood." *Worship* 46 (1972): 454–72.
Dockery, David S. "Southern Baptists in the Twenty-First Century." In *Southern Baptist Identity: An Evangelical Denomination Faces the Future*, edited by David S. Dockery, 13–21. Wheaton, IL: Crossway, 2009.

———. "The Role of Women in Worship and Ministry: Some Hermeneutical Questions." *Criswell Theological Review* 1 (1987): 363–86.

Donahue, John R. "'The Foolishness of God': New Testament Foundations for a Spirituality of the Priesthood." *Worship* 66 (1992): 517–35.

Donfried, Karl P. "A New Testament Scholar Looks at the Issue of Ministry." *Dialog* 27 (1988): 8–16.

Dragas, George D. "On the Priesthood and the Sacred Mysteries (Sacraments) According to St. Symeon of Thessalonica and Other Fathers." *Greek Orthodox Theological Review* 45 (2000): 525–52.

Duffy, Eamon. "The English Secular Clergy and the Counter-Reformation." *Journal of Ecclesiastical History* 34 (1983): 214–30.

Dulles, Avery. *Models of the Church*. Expanded ed. Garden City, NY: Doubleday, 1987.

Dunlap, E. Dale. "The Protestant Experience and Democratic Ecclesiology." In *A Democratic Catholic Church: The Reconstruction of Roman Catholicism*, edited by Eugene C. Bianchi and Rosemary Radford Ruether, 207–25. New York: Crossroad, 1992.

Durnbaugh, Donald F. *The Believers' Church: The History and Character of Radical Protestantism*. New York: Macmillan, 1968.

Eastwood, C. Cyril. "Luther's Conception of the Church." *Scottish Journal of Theology* 11 (1958): 22–36.

———. *The Priesthood of All Believers: An Examination of the Doctrine from the Reformation to the Present Day*. Minneapolis, MN: Augsburg, 1960; reprint, Eugene, OR: Wipf & Stock, 2009.

———. *The Royal Priesthood of the Faithful: An Investigation of the Doctrine from Biblical Times to the Reformation*. Minneapolis: Augsburg, 1960; reprint, Eugene, OR: Wipf & Stock, 2009.

Edge, Findley B. "Priesthood of Believers." *Review & Expositor* 60 (1963): 9–21.

Ellingworth, Paul. "The Unshakable Priesthood: Hebrews 7:24." *Journal for the Study of the New Testament* 23 (1985): 125–26.

Elliott, John Hall. "Death of a Slogan: From Royal Priests to Celebrating Community." *Una Sancta* 25 (1968): 18–31.

———. "Elders as Leaders in 1 Peter and the Early Church." *Currents in Theology and Mission* 28 (2001): 549–59.

Erickson, Millard J. *Christian Theology*. 2nd ed. Grand Rapids: Baker, 1998.

Erling, Bernhard. "Christian Believers: A Presbytery or a Sacerdocy?" *Dialog* 37 (1998): 230–31.

Estep, William R. *Baptists and Church Unity*. Nashville: Broadman, 1966.

Evans, Gillian R. *The Church and the Churches: Toward an Ecumenical Ecclesiology*. Cambridge: Cambridge University Press, 1994.

Evanson, Charles J. "The Office and Order of the Holy Ministry: Luther and Lutheran." In *And Every Tongue Confess: Essays in Honor of Norman Nagel on the Occasion of His Sixty-Fifth Birthday*, edited by Gerald S. Krispin and Jon D. Vieker, 153–78. Dearborn, MI: Nagel Festschrift Committee, 1990.

Felmy, Karl Christian. "Amt und Ordination im Gespräch mit der Orthodoxie." *Kerygma und Dogma* 52 (2006): 182–96.

Felton, Gayle C. "A Royal Priesthood in a New Millennium: The Ministry of the Baptized." *Quarterly Review* 20 (2000): 369–82.

Ferguson, Everett. *Baptism in the Early Church: History, Theology, and Liturgy in the First Five Centuries*. Grand Rapids: Eerdmans, 2009.

———. *The Church of Christ: A Biblical Ecclesiology for Today*. Grand Rapids: Eerdmans, 1996.

Fischer, Robert Harley. "Baptists and the Ministry: Luther on the Priesthood of All Believers." *Baptist Quarterly* 17 (1958): 293–411.

Flew, Robert Newton. *Jesus and His Church: A Study of the Idea of the Ecclesia in the New Testament*. London: Epworth, 1960.

Floor, Lambertus. "The General Priesthood of Believers in the Epistle to the Hebrews." In *Ad Hebraeos: Essays on the Epistle to the Hebrews*, 72–82. Pretoria, South Africa: Die Nuwe-Testamentiese Werkgemeenskap Van Suid-Afrika, 1971.

Fohrer, Georg. "Priester und Prophet: Amt und Charisma?" *Kerygma und Dogma* 17 (1971): 15–27.

Foley, Nadine, ed. *Preaching and the Non-Ordained: An Interdisciplinary Study*. Collegeville, MN: Liturgical Press, 1983.

Folsom, Marty. "The Trinity and Familia Ecclesiology." *Crux* 35 (1999): 12–18.

Forell, George W. "Baptism and the Universal Priesthood of Believers." *Trinity Seminary Review* 6 (1984): 34–40.

Forsyth, Peter T. *The Church and the Sacraments*. London: Independent Press, 1953.

Gaillardetz, Richard R. *Ecclesiology for a Global Church: A People Called and Sent*. Theology in Global Perspective Series. Maryknoll, NY: Orbis, 2008.

Galbreath, Paul. "Protestant Principles in Need of Reformation." *Perspectives* 7 (1992): 14–17.

Garrett, W. Barry. "Priesthood of Believers." In *Encyclopedia of Southern Baptists*, vol. 2. Nashville: Broadman, 1958.

Gelston, Anthony. "Royal Priesthood." *Evangelical Quarterly* 31 (1959): 152–63.

George, Timothy. "The Priesthood of All Believers." In *The People of God: Essays on the Believers' Church*, edited by Paul A. Basden and David S. Dockery, 85–95. Nashville: Broadman & Holman, 1991.

———. "The Priesthood of All Believers and the Quest for Theological Integrity." *Criswell Theological Review* 3 (1989): 283–94.

———. *Theology of the Reformers*. Nashville: Broadman & Holman, 1988.

Gerrish, Brian A. "Priesthood and Ministry in the Theology of Luther." *Church History* 34 (1965): 404–22.

Giles, Kevin. *What on Earth is the Church? An Exploration in New Testament Theology*. Downers Grove, IL: InterVarsity, 1995.

Gill, Theodore A. "Priesthood of Believers." *Theology Today* 15 (1958): 302–3.

Gillespie, Thomas W. "The Laity in Biblical Perspective." In *New Laity between Church and World*, edited by Ralph D. Bucy, 13–33. Waco, TX: Word Books, 1978.

Gleeson, Gerald P., ed. *Priesthood: The Hard Questions*. Newtown, Australia: E. J. Dwyer, 1993.

Gorevan, Patrick. "A People of Priests." In *The Mystery of Faith: Reflections on the Encyclical Ecclesia de Eucharistia*, edited by James J. McEvoy and Maurice P. Hogan, 161–72, 395. Blackrock, Ireland: Columba, 2005.

Grenz, Stanley J. "Biblical Priesthood and Women in Ministry." In *Discovering Biblical Equality: Complementarity without Hierarchy*, edited by Ronald W. Pierce and Rebecca Merrill Groothuis. Downers Grove, IL: InterVarsity, 2005.

Grieb, A Katherine. "People of God, Body of Christ, Koinonia of Spirit: The Role of Ethical Ecclesiology in Paul's 'Trinitarian' Language." *Anglican Theological Review*, 87 (2005): 225–52.

Grissom, Fred A, ed. "The Priesthood of Believers and Pastoral Authority." *Faith and Mission* 7 (1989): 2–60.

Grudem, Wayne A. "Wives Like Sarah, and the Husbands Who Honor Them." In *Recovering Biblical Manhood and Womanhood: A Response to Evangelical Feminism*, edited by John Piper and Wayne A. Grudem. Wheaton, IL: Crossway, 1991.

Guelzo, Allen C. "Are You a Priest: Luther Said Yes, Anglicans Hedged, and Southern Baptists Almost Split over the Question." *Christianity Today*, September 16, 1991, 35–38.

Gupta, Nijay. "A Spiritual House of Royal Priests, Chosen and Honored: The Presence and Function of Cultic Imagery in 1 Peter." *Perspectives in Religious Studies* 36 (2009): 61–76.

Halbrook, Jerry Dwain. "Case Studies of Selected Southern Baptist Churches That Have Adopted the Plural-Elder-Led Congregationalism Polity Model." DMin diss., Dallas Theological Seminary, 2007.

Hammett, John S. *Biblical Foundations for Baptist Churches: A Contemporary Ecclesiology*. Grand Rapids: Kregel, 2005.

———. "How Church and Parachurch Should Relate: Arguments for a Servant-Partnership Model." *Missiology* 28 (2000): 199–207.

———. "Regenerate Church Membership." In *Restoring Integrity in Baptist Churches*, edited by Thomas White, Jason G. Duesing, and Malcolm B. Yarnell, 21–43. Grand Rapids: Kregel, 2008.

Handspicker, M. B. "A Holy Priesthood." In *Laity in Ministry*, edited by George Peck and John S. Hoffman, 95–108. Valley Forge, PA: Judson, 1984.

Hardin, Reid D. "The 'Year of the Laity' in Southern Baptist Life." *Review & Expositor* 85 (1988): 669–79.

Harris, Maria. "Education for Priesthood." In *Education for Peace and Justice*, edited by Padraic O'Hare, 14–25. San Francisco: Harper and Row, 1983.

Hauerwas, Stanley, et al., eds. *The Wisdom of the Cross: Essays in Honor of John Howard Yoder*. Grand Rapids: Eerdmans, 1999.

Haymes, Brian, et al. *On Being the Church: Revisioning Baptist Identity*. Studies in Baptist History and Thought. Milton Keynes, U.K.: Paternoster, 2008.

Heim, S. Mark, ed. "Update on Baptism, Eucharist and Ministry." *American Baptist Quarterly* 7 (1988): 2–77.

Heintze, Gerhard. "Allgemeines Priestertum und Besonderes Amt." *Evangelische Theologie* 23 (1963): 617–46.

Hemphill, Tony. "The Practice of Infantile Baptism in Southern Baptist Churches and Subsequent Impact on Regenerate Church Membership." *Faith and Mission* 18 (2001): 74–87.

Hendel, Kurt K. "The Doctrine of the Ministry: The Reformation Heritage." *Currents in Theology and Mission* 17 (1990): 23–33.

Henderson, George D. "Priesthood of Believers." *Scottish Journal of Theology* 7 (1954): 1–15.

———. "Witness of the Laity." *Scottish Journal of Theology* 2 (1949): 174–86.

Herbert, Tim D. *Kenosis and Priesthood: Towards a Protestant Re-evaluation of the Ordained Ministry*. Milton Keynes, U.K.: Paternoster, 2008.

Heubach, Joachim. "Service and Services, Office and Offices, Pastor and Co-workers." *Lutheran Theological Journal* 12 (1978): 24–26.
Higginbotham, Joe, and Paul Patton. "The Battle for the Body." *Searching Together* 13 (1984): 29–34.
Hinds, Mark D. "Congregation as Educator: Problem and Possibility for the Professional Church Educator." *Religious Education* 95 (2000): 79–93.
Hinson, E. Glenn. "Pastoral Authority and the Priesthood of Believers from Cyprian to Calvin." *Faith and Mission* 7 (1989): 6–23.
Hintzen, Georg. "Das Gemeinsame Priestertum aller Gläubigen und das Besondere Priestertum des Dienstes in der Ökumenischen Diskussion." *Catholica* 45 (1991): 44–77.
Hobbs, Herschel H. *You Are Chosen: The Priesthood of All Believers.* San Francisco: Harper & Row, 1990.
Hök, Gösta. "Luther's Doctrine of the Ministry." *Scottish Journal of Theology* 7 (1954): 16–40.
Holland, Scott. "The Public Vocation of the Pastor." *Brethren Life and Thought* 46 (2001): 219–25.
Hong, Yong-gi. "Church and Mission: A Pentecostal Perspective." *International Review of Mission*, 90 (2001): 289–308.
Hopko, Thomas. "On the Male Character of Christian Priesthood." *St Vladimir's Theological Quarterly* 19 (1975): 147–73.
Horbury, William. "The Aaronic Priesthood in the Epistle to the Hebrews." *Journal for the Study of the New Testament* 19 (1983): 43–71.
Horrell, John Scott. *From the Ground Up: New Testament Foundations for the 21st Century Church.* Grand Rapids: Kregel, 2004.
Hoyer, George W. "Christianhood, Priesthood and Brotherhood." In *Accents in Luther's Theology: Essays in Commemoration of the 450th Anniversary of the Reformation*, edited by Heino O. Kadai, 148–98. St Louis, MO: Concordia, 1967.
Hunt, Anne. "Trinity and Church: Explorations in Ecclesiology from a Trinitarian Perspective." *Irish Theological Quarterly* 70 (2005): 215-35.
Hunt, Boyd. "New Dimensions in Church." In *New Dimensions in Evangelical Thought: Essays in Honor of Millard J. Erickson*, edited by David S. Dockery, 338–53. Downers Grove, IL: InterVarsity, 1998.
Hussey, M. Edmund. "What Is a Priest?" In *American Catholic Identity: Essays in an Age of Change*, edited by Francis J. Butler, 95–107. Kansas City, MO: Sheed & Ward, 1994.
Johnson, John E. "The Old Testament Offices as Paradigm for Pastoral Identity." *Bibliotheca Sacra* 152 (1995): 182–200.
Johnson, Robert C. "Ordination and Ministry." *Church & Society* 67 (1977): 40–58.
Jones, Greg. "On the Priesthood." *Anglican Theological Review* 91 (2009): 47–60.
Jones, Mary Elizabeth. "The Priesthood of the Believer in the Public Square: Religious Conviction, Political Choice, and Fundamentalism in the Southern Baptist Convention." PhD diss., University of Massachusetts Amherst, 2002.
Kärkkäinen, Veli-Matti. *An Introduction to Ecclesiology: Ecumenical, Historical, & Global Perspectives.* Downers Grove, IL: InterVarsity, 2002.
———. "The Calling of the Whole People of God into Ministry: The Spirit, Church, and Laity." *Studia Theologica* 53 (1999): 144–62.

Karpp, Heinrich. "Der Laie als Bibelleser und Predigthörer." In *Vom Amt des Laien in Kirche und Theologie: Festschrift für Gerhard Krause zum 70. Geburtstag*, edited by Henning Schröer and Gerhard Müller, 357–71. New York: Walter De Gruyter, 1982.

Kjeseth, Peter Lars. "Baptism as Ordination." *Dialog* 8 (1969): 177–82.

Knellwolf, Ulrich. "Überlegungen zum Allgemeinen Priestertum." *Reformatio* 32 (1983): 412–14.

Korby, Kenneth. "The Pastoral Office and the Priesthood of Believers." In *Lord Jesus Christ, Will You Not Stay: Essays in Honor of Ronald Feuerhahn on the Occasion of His Sixty-Fifth Birthday*, edited by Ronald R. Feuerhahn and J. Bart Day, 333–71. Houston, TX: Feuerhahn Festschrift Committee, 2002.

Kowalchuk, Allan D. "The Participation of the Laity in the Church." *Patristic and Byzantine Review* 3 (1984): 113–21.

Kühn, Ulrich. "Allgemeines Priestertum, Amt und Episkopé: Zum Beitrag von Ulrich Körtner." *Kerygma und Dogma* 52 (2006): 94–97.

Küng, Hans. *The Church*. Garden City, NY: Image Books, 1976.

Kung, Lap-yan. "Priesthood of All Believers and Rights of All Humans." *Jian Dao* 10 (1998): 59–80.

Kurien, Jacob. "Church Unity—Claiming a Common Future: An Orthodox Perspective." *Ecumenical Review* 58 (2006): 118–20.

Lakeland, Paul. "The Laity." In *Routledge Companion to the Christian Church*, edited by Gerard Mannion and Lewis S. Mudge, 511–23. London: Routledge, 2008.

Lampe, G. W. H. "Ministerial Priesthood." *Modern Churchman* 5 (1962): 200–11.

Lange, Armin, and Arne Dembek. "Ordination für Alle? Ein Rheinischer Sonderweg—Reformatorische Konsequenz oder Theologisch-Kirchenpolitischer Kurzschluss?" *Evangelische Theologie* 67 (2007): 233–39.

Lash, Nicholas, and Joseph Rhymer, eds. "A Joint Anglican and Methodist Statement about Priesthood and Ministry." In *The Christian Priesthood*, 77–81. Denville, NJ: Dimension, 1970.

Lea, Thomas D. "The Priesthood of All Christians according to the New Testament." *Southwestern Journal of Theology* 30 (1988): 15–21.

Lehenbauer, Joel D. "The Priesthood of All Saints." *Missio Apostolica* 9 (2001): 4–17.

Leithart, Peter J. "Christs Christened into Christ: Priesthood and Initiation in Augustine and Aquinas." *Studia Liturgica* 29 (1999): 68–83.

———. *The Baptized Body*. Moscow, ID: Canon, 2007.

———. *The Priesthood of the Plebs: A Theology of Baptism*. Eugene, OR: Wipf & Stock, 2003.

———. "Womb of the World: Baptism and the Priesthood of the New Covenant in Hebrews 10:19–22." *Journal for the Study of the New Testament* 78 (2000): 49–65.

LeMasters, Philip. *Discipleship between Creation and Redemption: Toward a Believers' Church and Social Ethic*. Lanham, MD: University Press of America, 1997.

Lennan, Richard. "Rahner's Theology of the Priesthood and the Development of Doctrine." *Philosophy & Theology* 12 (2000): 155–85.

Leonard, Bill J. "The Church." In *Has Our Theology Changed? Southern Baptist Thought since 1845*, edited by Paul A. Basden, 159–79. Nashville: Broadman & Holman, 1994.

Lesher, William E. "Ordering of Ministries of All the Baptized People of God." *Currents in Theology and Mission* 17 (1990): 57–65.

Lewis, Richard Wyman. "The Rule of Christ and Congregational Polity: A Unique Challenge and Opportunity." *Southwestern Journal of Theology* 47 (2004): 45–53.

Littell, Franklin H. *The Anabaptist View of the Church: A Study in the Origins of Sectarian Protestantism.* 2nd ed. Boston: Starr King, 1958.

Lofthouse, William Frederick. "Priesthood of Believers." *Congregational Quarterly* 36 (1958): 6–13.

Lorenzen, Thorwald. "Baptism and Church Membership: Some Baptist Positions and Their Ecumenical Implications." *Journal of Ecumenical Studies* 18 (1981): 561–74.

Luther, Martin. "An Open Letter to the Christian Nobility of the German Nation concerning the Reform of the Christian Estate." In *Works of Martin Luther*, trans. Charles M. Jacobs. Vol. 2. Philadelphia: A. J. Holman, 1915. Accessed September 9, 2011. Online: http://www.iclnet.org/pub/resources/text/wittenberg/luther/web/nblty-01.html.

———. *Martin Luther's Basic Theological Writings.* 2nd ed. Minneapolis: Fortress, 2005.

Maize, Gregory Lynn. "Doctrines in Conflict? The Priesthood of the Believer and Pastoral Authority." DMin diss., Reformed Theological Seminary, 1999.

Manley, Ken. *The Baptist World Alliance and Inter-Church Relationship.* Baptist Heritage and Identity Series. Falls Church, VA: Baptist World Alliance, 2003.

Manson, Thomas Walter. *Ministry and Priesthood: Christ's and Ours; Two Lectures.* London: Epworth, 1958.

Marshall, John S. "'A Spiritual House an Holy Priesthood' (1 Peter ii.5)." *Anglican Theological Review* 28 (1946): 227–28.

Mayer, Rolph. "The Confessions, the Public Ministry, and the Ordination of Women." *Lutheran Theological Journal* 31 (1997): 82–88.

McBain, L. Doward. "Clergy-Lay Issues and Relations: The Baptist Perspective." *Foundations* 15 (1972): 156–62.

McClendon, James William. *Doctrine.* Nashville: Abingdon, 1995.

McCormick, K. Steve. "The Church an Icon of the Holy Trinity? A Spirit-Christology as Necessary Prolegomena of Ecclesiology." *Wesleyan Theological Journal* 41 (2006): 227–41.

McDonald, Durstan R., ed. "Theology of Priesthood: A Consultation." *Anglican Theological Review* 9 (1984): 1–121.

McKim, Donald K. "Worship." In *Westminster Dictionary of Theological Terms*, 307. Louisville, KY: Westminster John Knox, 1996.

McLennan, W. E. "The Place and Work of the Laity in the Church." *Methodist Review* 84 (1902): 924–38.

McNeal, Reggie. "The Priesthood of All Believers." In *Has Our Theology Changed? Southern Baptist Thought since 1845*, edited by Paul A. Basden, 204–29. Nashville: Broadman & Holman, 1994.

Merkle, Benjamin L. *40 Questions about Elders and Deacons.* Grand Rapids: Kregel, 2008.

Meyer, Carl S. "Apostolicity and Ministry: A Lutheran View." *Concordia Theological Monthly* 43 (1972): 77–93.

Migliore, Daniel L. "The Communion of the Triune God: Towards a Trinitarian Ecclesiology in Reformed Perspective." In *Reformed Theology: Identity and Ecumenicity*, edited by Wallace M. Alston Jr. and Michael Welker, 140–54. Grand Rapids: Eerdmans, 2003.

Mikolaski, Samuel J. "The Contemporary Relevance of the Priesthood of All Christians." *Southwestern Journal of Theology* 30 (1988): 6–14.

Minear, Paul S. *Images of the Church in the New Testament.* Philadelphia: Westminster, 1960.

Moberly, Robert Campbell. *Ministerial Priesthood: Chapters (Preliminary to a Study of the Ordinal) on the Rationale of Ministry and the Meaning of Christian Priesthood.* 2nd ed. London: SPCK, 1969.

Mohler, R. Albert Jr. "Southern Baptist Identity: Is There a Future?" In *Southern Baptist Identity: An Evangelical Denomination Faces the Future,* edited by David S. Dockery. Wheaton, IL: Crossway, 2009.

Moingt, Joseph. "Authority and Ministry." *Journal of Ecumenical Studies* 19 (1982): 202–25.

Moltmann, Jürgen. *The Church in the Power of the Spirit: A Contribution to Messianic Ecclesiology.* New York: Harper & Row, 1977; reprint, London: SCM, 1992.

Monhollen, Steven A. "Ministry on the Margins: Themes for Understanding Disciples Ministry." *Lexington Theological Quarterly* 41 (2006): 201–13.

Montover, Nathan. "The Political and Temporal Dimensions of Luther's Doctrine of the Priesthood of All Believers: A Case Study." PhD diss., Lutheran School of Theology at Chicago, 2008.

Moore, Allen J. "Pastoral Teaching: A Revisionist View." *Quarterly Review* 3 (1983): 63–76.

Morrison, John D. "Trinity and Church: An Examination of Theological Methodology." *Journal of the Evangelical Theological Society* 40 (1997): 445–54.

Müller, Gerhard. "Allgemeines Priestertum aller Getauften und Kirchliches Amt in der Reformationszeit." *Kerygma und Dogma* 52 (2006): 98–104.

Muthiah, Robert. "A Practical Theology of the Royal Priesthood: Trinitarian Ecclesiology, Institutions of Postmodernity, and Congregational Practices in Dialogue." PhD diss., Fuller Theological Seminary, 2005.

———. "Christian Practices, Congregational Leadership, and the Priesthood of All Believers." *Journal of Religious Leadership* 2 (2003): 167–203.

———. *The Priesthood of All Believers in the Twenty-First Century.* Eugene, OR: Pickwick, 2009.

Nagel, Norman E. "Luther and the Priesthood of All Believers." *Concordia Theological Quarterly* 61 (1997): 277–98.

Neamtu, Andrew. "The Priesthood of All Believers and Authority in the Church." *Faith and Mission* 17 (2000): 40–51.

Nellas, Panayiotis. "The Ministry of the Laity." In *Martyria/Mission: The Witness of the Orthodox Churches Today,* edited by Ion Bria, 60–65. Geneva: World Council of Churches, 1980.

Newbigin, Lesslie. *The Reunion of the Church: A Defence of the South India Scheme.* 2nd ed. London: SCM, 1960.

———. *Trinitarian Doctrine for Today's Mission.* Carlisle, UK: Paternoster, 1998.

Newell, Samuel W. "Many Members: The Relation of the Individual to the People of God." *Interpretation* 5 (1951): 413–26.

Newman, Elizabeth. "The Priesthood of All Believers and the Necessity of the Church." In *Recycling the Past or Researching History? Studies in Baptist Historiography and Myths,* edited by Philip E. Thompson and Anthony R. Cross, 50–66. Milton Keynes, UK: Paternoster, 2005.

Noll, Mark A. "Believer-Priests in the Church: Luther's View." *Christianity Today,* October 26, 1973, 4–8.

———. "Landmarkism." In *Evangelical Dictionary of Theology,* edited by Walter A. Elwell. 2nd ed., 669-70. Grand Rapids: Baker, 2001.

Nordenhaug, Josef. "Baptists and a Regenerate Church Membership." *Review & Expositor* 60 (1963): 149–60.
Norman, Stanton R. "Southern Baptist Identity: A Theological Perspective." In *Southern Baptist Identity: An Evangelical Denomination Faces the Future*, edited by David S. Dockery, 43–63. Wheaton, IL: Crossway, 2009.
Norris, Richard A. "The Beginnings of Christian Priesthood." *Anglican Theological Review* 9 (1984): 18–32.
O'Collins, Gerald, and Michael Keena Jones. *Jesus Our Priest: A Christian Approach to the Priesthood of Christ*. New York: Oxford University Press, 2010.
Ogden, Greg. *Unfinished Business: Returning the Ministry to the People of God*. Rev. ed. Grand Rapids: Zondervan, 2003.
Orr, David. "Educating for the Priesthood of the Faithful." *Worship* 83 (2009): 431–57.
———. "The Giving of the Priesthood to the Faithful." In *Priesthood: The Hard Questions*, edited by Gerald P. Gleeson, 61–77. Newtown, Australia: E. J. Dwyer, 1993.
Osterhaven, M. Eugene. "Renewal in Congregational Life." *Reformed Review* 22 (1969): 16–26.
Palmer, Paul F. "The Lay Priesthood: Real or Metaphorical?" *Theological Studies* 8 (1947): 574–613.
Parente, Pietro. "Baptism." In *Dictionary of Dogmatic Theology*, 29–31. Milwaukee: Bruce, 1951.
Patterson, Paige. "The Meaning of Authority in the Local Church." In *Recovering Biblical Manhood and Womanhood: A Response to Evangelical Feminism*, edited by John Piper and Wayne Grudem, 248–51. Wheaton, IL: Crossway, 1991.
———. *So You've Been Called to a Church*. Wake Forest, NC: Magnolia Hill Papers, 1996.
Patton, Richard D. "Baptists and Regenerate Church Membership: Historical Perspective and Present Practice." *Baptist History and Heritage* 13 (1978): 28–32.
Patzia, Arthur G. "Baby Dedication in the Believers' Church." *American Baptist Quarterly* 3 (1984): 63–72.
Paul, Robert S. *Ministry*. Grand Rapids: Eerdmans, 1965.
Peterson, C. Richard. "Lutherans, Episcopalians and the Priesthood of All Believers." *Lutheran Forum* 32 (1998): 22–26.
Pfitzner, Victor C. "'General Priesthood' and Ministry." *Lutheran Theological Journal* 5 (1971): 97–110.
Phillips, Robert L. "Pastoral Authority and the Doctrine of the Priesthood of Believers in a Congregation." *Faith and Mission* 7 (1989): 46–60.
Pinson, William M. "Baptists: The Priesthood of the Believer or of Believers?" In *Baptist Distinctives*. Dallas, TX: Baptist Standard, 2005. Accessed September 10, 2011. Online: http://baptistdistinctives.org/artpdf/article7_4_04_05.pdf.
Piper, John, and Wayne A. Grudem, eds. *Recovering Biblical Manhood and Womanhood: A Response to Evangelical Feminism*. Wheaton, IL: Crossway, 1991.
Pitts, William L. "Arguing Regenerate Church Membership: Baptist Identity during Its First Decade, 1610–1620." *Baptist History and Heritage* 44 (2009): 20–39.
———. "The Relation of Baptists to Other Churches." In *The People of God: Essays on the Believers' Church*, edited by Paul A. Basden and David S. Dockery, 205–50. Nashville: Broadman & Holman, 1991.
Pool, Jeff B. "Baptist Infidelity to the Principle of Religious Liberty." *Perspectives in Religious Studies* 17 (1990): 13–30.

Preus, Herman A. "Luther on the Universal Priesthood and the Office of the Ministry." *Concordia Journal* 5 (1979): 55–62.
Ratzinger, Joseph. "Biblical Foundations of Priesthood." *Communio* 17 (1990): 617–27.
Rees, Frank D. "The Worship of All Believers." *Baptist Quarterly* 41 (2005): 175–89.
"Resolution on the Priesthood of the Believer." Southern Baptist Convention, 1988. Accessed September 10, 2011. Online: http://www.sbc.net/resolutions/amResolution.asp?ID=872.
Reumann, John H. P. "Ordained Minister and Layman in Lutheranism." In *Eucharist and Ministry*, edited by Paul C. Empie and T. Austin Murphy, 227–82. Minneapolis: Augsburg, 1979.
Richardson, Wyman L. *Walking Together: A Congregational Reflection on Biblical Church Discipline*. Eugene, OR: Wipf & Stock, 2007.
Robinson, William. *Completing the Reformation: The Doctrine of the Priesthood of All Believers*. Lexington, KY: The College of the Bible, 1955.
Rohls, Jan. "Das Geistliche Amt in der Reformatorischen Theologie." *Kerygma und Dogma* 31 (1985): 135–61.
Ronaldson, Kathlyn, and Murray D. Gow, eds. "Priests One and All: The Priestly Ministry of Christ and the Church." *Journal of the Christian Brethren Research Fellowship* 129 (1992): 7–43.
Rosato, Philip J. "Priesthood of the Baptized and Priesthood of the Ordained: Complementary Approaches to Their Interrelation." *Gregorianum* 68 (1987): 215–66.
Ross, John M. "The Priesthood of All Believers." *Expository Times* 63 (1951): 45–48.
Rowell, J. B. "Our Great High Priest." *Bibliotheca Sacra* 118 (1961): 148–53.
Rue, Victoria. "Crossroads: Women Priests in the Roman Catholic Church." *Feminist Theology* 17 (2008): 11–20.
Ruiz, Jerjes. "The Priesthood of All Believers." In *Faith Born in the Struggle for Life: A Rereading of Protestant Faith in Latin America Today*, edited by Dow Kirkpatrick, translated by Lewistine McCoy, 98–115. Grand Rapids: Eerdmans, 1988.
Russell, D. S. "The Ministry and Sacraments." *Baptist Quarterly* 17 (1957): 67–73.
Scharen, Christian Batalden. "Subject to Discipline: Authority, Sexuality, and the Production of Candidates for Ordained Ministry." *Journal of the American Academy of Religion* 66 (1998): 313–44.
Schäufele, Wolfgang. "Missionary Vision and Activity of the Anabaptist Laity." *Mennonite Quarterly Review* 36 (1962): 99–115.
Schroeer, Henning. "Die Theologische Kompetenz des Laien im Kirchenleitenden Handeln." In *Vom Amt des Laien in Kirche und Theologie: Festschrift für Gerhard Krause zum 70. Geburtstag*, edited by Henning Schröer and Gerhard Müller, 320–42. New York: Walter De Gruyter, 1982.
Schurb, Ken. "Church and Ministry." *Logia* 16 (2007): 25–29.
Schweizer, Eduard. "Glaubensgrundlage und Glaubenserfahrung in der Kirche des Allgemeinen Priestertums: 1 Petr 2,1–10." In *Kirche und Volk Gottes: Festschrift für Jürgen Roloff zum 70. Geburtstag*, edited by Martin Karrer, Wolfgang Kraus, and Otto Merk, 272–83. Neukirchen-Vluyn: Neukirchener, 2000.
———. "The Priesthood of All Believers: 1 Peter 2:1–10." In *Worship, Theology and Ministry in the Early Church: Essays in Honor of Ralph P. Martin*, edited by Michael J. Wilkins and Terence Paige, 285–93. Sheffield: JSOT, 1992.

Scott, William M. F. "Priesthood in the New Testament." *Scottish Journal of Theology* 10 (1957): 399–415.
Sehested, Nancy Hastings. "Women and Ministry in the Local Congregation." *Review & Expositor* 83 (1986): 71–79.
Sell, Alan P. F. "Doctrine, Polity, Liberty: What Do Baptists Stand For?" In *Pilgrim Pathways: Essays in Baptist History in Honor of B. R. White*, edited by William H. Brackney, Paul S. Fiddes, and John H. Y. Briggs, 1–46. Macon, GA: Mercer University Press, 1999.
Shirley, Chris. "It Takes a Church to Make a Disciple: An Integrative Model of Discipleship for the Church." *Southwestern Journal of Theology* 50 (2008): 207–23.
Shurden, Walter B., ed. *Proclaiming the Baptist Vision: The Priesthood of All Believers.* Macon, GA: Smyth & Helwys, 1993.
———. *The Doctrine of the Priesthood of Believers.* Nashville: Convention, 1987.
———. "The Priesthood of All Believers and Pastoral Authority in Baptist Thought." *Faith and Mission* 7 (1989): 24–45.
Silva, Gilberto da. "The Lutheran Church as a Church of Mission against the Background of the Priesthood of All Believers." *Missio Apostolica* 14 (2006): 21–27.
Smith, Almer J. *The Making of the 1963 Baptist Faith and Message.* Eugene, OR: Wipf & Stock, 2008.
Smith, Michael K. "The Universal Priesthood: An Exegesis of 1 Peter 2:1–10" (originally prepared for the ELS General Pastoral Conference held at the Marvin M. Schwan Retreat and Conference Center, Trego, WI, 1 October 2002). Accessed September 10, 2011. Online: http://www.blts.edu/wp-content/uploads/2011/06/MKS-Priesthood.pdf.
Smith, Robert S. "A 'Second Reformation'! 'Office' and 'Charisma' in the New Testament." *Reformed Theological Review* 58 (1999): 151–62.
Spinks, Bryan D. "The Liturgical Ministry of the Laity." In *Kingdom of Priests: Liturgical Formation of the People of God, Papers Read at the International Anglican Liturgical Consultation, Brixen, North Italy, 24–25 August 1987*, edited by Thomas J. Talley, 20–27. Bramcote, England: Grove, 1988.
Spitz, Lewis William. "The Universal Priesthood of Believers with Luther's Comments." *Concordia Theological Monthly* 23 (1952): 1–15.
Stewart, Cheryl A. "Integrity in the Priesthood of All Believers." In *Theology and the Black Experience: The Lutheran Heritage Interpreted by African and African-American Theologians*, edited by Albert Pero and Ambrose Moyo, 170–93. Minneapolis: Augsburg, 1988.
Strege, Merle D. *Baptism and Church: A Believers' Church Vision.* Grand Rapids: Sagamore, 1986.
Stylianopoulos, Theodore G. "Holy Eucharist and Priesthood in the New Testament." *Greek Orthodox Theological Review* 23 (1978): 113–30.
Sweeney, Douglas A. "On the Vocation of Historians to the Priesthood of Believers: Faithful Practices in Service of the Guild." *Fides et Historia* 39 (2007): 1–13.
Tamney, Joseph B., and Stephen D. Johnson. "The Popularity of Strict Churches." *Review of Religious Research* 39 (1998): 209–23.
Taylor, Ruth Mattson. "Needed: A Re-Emphasis on the Universal Priesthood of All Believers." *Dialog* 30 (1991): 326–30.
Techau, Donna R. "The Waters of the Womb: Towards a Theology of Maternal Priesthood." *ARC* 30 (2002): 85–99.

Teigen, Erling. "The Universal Priesthood in the Lutheran Confessions." *Logia* (October 1992): 9–15.

Thomas, W. H. Griffith. "Is the New Testament Minister a Priest?" *Bibliotheca Sacra* 136 (1979): 65–73.

Todd, John M. "The Apostolate of the Laity." *Downside Review* 70 (1952): 150–62.

Torrance, James B. "The Vicarious Humanity and Priesthood of Christ in the Theology of John Calvin." In *Calvinus Ecclesiae Doctor*, edited by Wilhelm H. Neuser, 69–84. Kampen, Netherlands: J. H. Kok, 1980.

Torrance, Thomas F. *Royal Priesthood: A Theology of Ordained Ministry*. 2nd ed. London: T & T Clark, 2003.

Tuttle, Robert G. Jr. "The Priesthood of All Believers in the Postmodern Congregation." In *Grace and Holiness in a Changing World: A Wesleyan Proposal for Postmodern Ministry*, edited by Jeffrey E. Greenway and Joel B. Green, 85–94. Nashville: Abingdon, 2007.

Unnatha, Sister. "The Apostolic Succession of the Church and Ecumenism." *Christian Orient* 28 (2007): 169–78.

Valantasis, Richard. "Body, Hierarchy, and Leadership in Chrysostom's on the Priesthood." *Greek Orthodox Theological Review* 30 (1985): 455–71.

Valeta, Dave. "The Priesthood of All Believers and the Pastor." *Searching Together* 11 (1982): 28–34.

Van der Kooij, Arie. "A Kingdom of Priests: Comment on Exodus 19:6." In *Interpretation of Exodus: Studies in Honour of Cornelis Houtman*, edited by Riemer Roukema, 171–79. Dudley, MA: Peeters, 2006.

———. "The Greek Bible and Jewish Concepts of Royal Priesthood and Priestly Monarchy." In *Jewish Perspectives on Hellenistic Rulers*, edited by Tessa Rajak, Sarah Pearce, James Aitken, and Jennifer Dines, 255–64. Berkeley: University of California Press, 2008.

Van Gelder, Craig. "Rethinking Denominations and Denominationalism in Light of a Missional Ecclesiology." *Word & World* 25 (2005): 23–33.

Volf, Miroslav. *After Our Likeness: The Church as the Image of the Trinity*. Grand Rapids: Eerdmans, 1998.

Watson, Philip S. "Priesthood and Ministry." *London Quarterly and Holborn Review* 182 (1957): 211–16; 305–7.

Weaver, J. Denny. "A Believers' Church Christology." *Mennonite Quarterly Review* 57 (1983): 112–31.

Wengert, Timothy J. *Priesthood, Pastors, Bishops: Public Ministry for the Reformation and Today*. Minneapolis: Fortress, 2008.

Wenz, Armin, and Holger Sonntag. "The Argument over Women's Ordination in Lutheranism as a Paradigmatic Conflict of Dogma." *Concordia Theological Quarterly* 71 (2007): 319–46.

West, W. Morris S. "The Child and the Church: A Baptist Perspective." In *Pilgrim Pathways: Essays in Baptist History in Honor of B. R. White*, edited by William H. Brackney, Paul S. Fiddes, and John H. Y. Briggs, 75–110. Macon, GA: Mercer University Press, 1999.

White, Thomas, Jason G. Duesing, and Malcolm B. Yarnell, eds. *First Freedom: The Baptist Perspective on Religious Liberty*. Nashville: B & H, 2007.

White, Thomas, Jason G. Duesing, and Malcolm B. Yarnell, eds. *Restoring Integrity in Baptist Churches*. Grand Rapids: Kregel, 2008.

Wilckens, Ulrich. "Kirchliches Amt und Gemeinsames Priestertum aller Getauften im Blick auf die Kirchenverfassungen der Lutherischen Kirchen." *Kerygma und Dogma* 52 (2006): 25–57.

Williams, George Huntston. "Reluctance to Inform." *Theology Today* 14 (1957): 229–55.

Wills, Gregory A. *Democratic Religion: Freedom, Authority, and Church Discipline in the Baptist South, 1785–1900.* Religion in America Series. New York: Oxford University Press, 1997.

———. "Southern Baptists and Church Discipline." In *Restoring Integrity in Baptist Churches,* edited by Thomas White, Jason G. Duesing, and Malcolm B. Yarnell, 179–97. Grand Rapids: Kregel, 2008.

Winward, Stephen Frederick. "The Church in the New Testament." In *The Pattern of the Church: A Baptist View,* edited by Alec Gilmore. London: Lutterworth, 1963.

Wriedt, Markus. "Luther on Call and Ordination: A Look at Luther and the Ministry." *Concordia Journal* 28 (2002): 254–69.

Wright, Nigel G. "Inclusive Representation: Towards a Doctrine of Christian Ministry." *Baptist Quarterly* 39 (2001): 159–74.

Yarnell, Malcolm B., III. "Changing Baptist Concepts of Royal Priesthood." In *The Rise of the Laity in Evangelical Protestantism,* edited by Deryck W. Lovegrove, 236–52. New York: Routledge, 2002.

———. "Congregational Priesthood and the *Inventio* or Invention of Authority." *Journal for Baptist Theology and Ministry* 3 (2005): 110–35.

———. *Formation of Christian Doctrine.* Nashville: B & H, 2007.

———. "From Christological Ecclesiology to Functional Ecclesiasticism: Developments in Southern Baptist Understandings of the Nature and Role of the Churches." Paper presented to Anglican Communion-Baptist World Alliance International Theological Conversations, Wolfville, Nova Scotia, September 11, 2003.

———. "Oikos Theou: A Theologically Neglected but Important Ecclesiological Metaphor." *Midwestern Journal of Theology* 2 (2003): 53–65.

———. "Royal Priesthood in the English Reformation." PhD diss., University of Oxford, 2000.

———. "The Priesthood of Believers: Rediscovering the Biblical Doctrine of Royal Priesthood." In *Restoring Integrity in Baptist Churches,* edited by Thomas White, John G. Duesing, and Malcolm B. Yarnell, 221–44. Grand Rapids: Kregel, 2008.

———. "The Reformation Development of the Priesthood of All Believers." ThM thesis, Duke University, 1996.

Yoder, John Howard. "The Believers' Church Conferences in Historical Perspective." *Mennonite Quarterly Review* 65 (1991): 5–19.

———. *The Priestly Kingdom: Social Ethics as Gospel.* Notre Dame, IN: University of Notre Dame, 1984.

———. *The Royal Priesthood: Essays Ecclesiological and Ecumenical,* edited by Michael G. Cartwright. Scottdale, PA: Herald, 1998.

Young, J. Terry. "Baptists and the Priesthood of Believers." *Theological Educator: A Journal of Theology and Ministry* 53 (1996): 19–29.

www.ingramcontent.com/pod-product-compliance
Lightning Source LLC
Chambersburg PA
CBHW071857160426
43197CB00013B/2515